WIGGLES, WINKS & WIZARDS

Paul & Kerby's Great Adventure

Paul H. D. Rothfuss

R|L Publishing, LLC
Alachua, FL • Minneapolis, MN

———

R|L Publishing, LLC
3524 Fourteenth Avenue South
Minneapolis, Minnesota 55407
WWW.RLPUBLISHERS.COM
612.840.2412

———

Throughout this book you will find scannable QR codes in conjunction with hyperlinks. These have been provided for the reader's convenience. If the book is being read on a device that is not connected to the internet, a smartphone or tablet with a QR scanner can be used to immediately access the link and continue the reader's experience with the book. Some smart phones can scan QR codes through the camera, and free QR scanners are available at your favorite app store.

All photos, images and recordings used in this book are the property of Paul H. D. Rothfuss, RL Publishing, LLC, any individual copyright holder as noted, or public domain.

Original Cover Art by:
Todd Hollingsworth, artist
T&T Design (ttcreative.us)

ISBN: 978-1-7321623-3-4 (WWW eBook)
ISBN: 978-1-7321623-4-1 (WWW POD)
ISBN: 978-1-7321623-5-8 (WWW Audiobook)

Other Books By The Author

"ALIAS EMPEROR RODGERS: A Majestic Memoir by Baltimore's Emperor of Insanity In The Crazy Daze of '60's Top 40 Radio" (published April, 2018)

To Barbie, Maria and Dorothy

CONTENTS

INTRODUCTION

Can childhood dreams come true? We all have them. The answer is yes if you are Paul Rothfuss and Kerby Confer. Their climb to the top of the broadcast mountain serves as an inspiration for all who dream of one day realizing their own dreams.

Two childhood friends as different in make-up and personality as day and night band together, first as Top 40 disc jockeys in the Golden Days of Rock & Roll and then as major players in radio station ownership and operation. 'Who are these guys and how and why did they succeed' is addressed in the pages to follow.

I met the dynamic duo post DJ glory days. Kerby telephoned my law office and arranged an in-person meeting to discuss their ownership plans and to ascertain if my firm was right for their newly formed Keystone Broadcasting Company (later re-named Keymarket Communications). Such meetings generally last an hour or two with each party selling the other on why they should get together.

The charismatic smiling Kerby and the cantankerous risk-taking Paul won me over in a matter of four compelling hours. I learned that we had a lot in common, particularly the need to succeed—yes, all three of us were compulsive over-achievers. At day's end I became Keymarket's go-to Attorney and voice at the FCC.

I was a jock in high school and college, lettering in three sports, but I "blew out" my knee in a summer league game that ended my big league dreams. So off I went to Law School in Washington, D.C. after which I started my professional career working at the Federal Communications Commission.

Three years later it was time to move on. I entered private practice specializing in media and entertainment law with a goal of having my own law firm by age 35.

So back to Paul and Kerby. The task at hand was three fold: identify desired cities, find available stations and then come up with the dollars to finalize the acquisition. The story about how Paul and Kerby went about assembling their chain of radio stations and making each one a profit center will enlighten and entertain all.

Each purchase brought its own unique business and FCC challenges for me to solve but as Paul would always remind me - "That's why we pay you the big bucks"! We never failed to consummate a transaction but there were plenty of anxious moments!

The best news? Every so often the "good guys" do win and Paul and Kerby won big! The dollars matched the accolades that poured in over the years as Keymarket grew into a major player in the radio industry. Yet while fame and fortune grew for Paul and Kerby, they never changed. Loyalty to family and friends remained a top priority. The reward for me is a friendship going on 45 years, one that still brings a smile to my face.

Contrary to popular belief, there are no important lawyers - important clients make lawyers important. So to Paul and Kerby: congratulations on your success and thank you for helping me to reach the top of my profession.

And most of all thank you for your continued friendship.
—Jason L. Shrinsky, Esq.

PREFACE

"WIGGLES, WINKS & WIZARDS: Paul and Kerby's Great Adventure" would not be possible without the boyhood pledge and the rich on-air life of Paul *(Emperor Rodgers)* Rothfuss and Kerby *(Kerby Scott)* Confer who met at age 12 (1952) while performing in a Christmas play at Thaddeus Stevens Junior High School. Their radio 'life partnership' would begin six years later, in June, 1958.

—Frank Jovis

The 'anything goes...no-holds-barred' days of Top 40 Radio seem so long ago and far away, but it's from those very days that Kerby and I emerged to become successful radio entrepreneurs.

"WIGGLES, WINKS & WIZARDS: ..." is a business book, but it is by no means a '"How To" or a 'step-by-step' instructional. That approach would have been dishonest...and boring.

Kerby and I weren't formally trained in how to run a successful radio station. Instead our 'formal education' came via years of keenly observing how the experts for whom we worked were doing things ... hands on and day-to-day ... the kind of education unavailable in the classroom.

For Starters

As detailed in my previous book, *"ALIAS EMPEROR RODGERS: ...,"* Kerby and I made a vow at age eighteen: "Someday we're going to own a radio station together." 'The Vow' was 'top-of-mind' for us for many years - we spoke it to each other often.

Because of The Vow, we always paid close attention to the stations' managers and sales managers during our years on the air. Although they were unaware, we'd 'apprenticed ourselves' to these good people and were privileged to see first-hand what worked and what did not.

As time passed it became clear: The 'key to success' for these stations (and for their advertisers) lay in the ability to get noticed. Truth is, 'Getting Noticed' was the reason behind the crazy, whacky stunts that radio stations did in those days - the *only* reason.

No one ever spoke the words 'get noticed' to us, but the evidence was compelling and the use of the strategy so pervasive, the only way we could have missed it was if we'd been asleep. We were not asleep.

In a nutshell: 'Getting noticed', and doing so in ways that were easy for folks to remember and enjoy, is the main reason for the success we were to achieve.

To the radio stations we purchased we added 'get noticed' to the same 'anything goes' attitude we acquired during our early days, first as we 're-imaged' the stations and then as step-by-step we took most of them from afterthoughts to the top of the ratings in their markets.

Food For Thought

"We become what we think about." —Earl Nightingale, Motivational Speaker

"When you love something it will give you all of its secrets." — Bob Parsons, Founder - Go Daddy

The Earl Nightingale quote is the underpinning of his world-famous lecture titled "The Strangest Secret." In January of 1973 Kerby gave me a cassette of this lecture. It changed my life.

Thirty-one years later, in 2004, I heard the Bob Parsons quote when I stumbled across an online talk he was giving. Truer words were never spoken.

It was this kind of thinking that was driving us to succeed.

Ownership was our goal. We loved radio - and it gave us all of its secrets.

So *"WIGGLES, WINKS & WIZARDS: ..."* is about what can happen when one finds something that interests them, then plunges in and gives it their all – learning as much about it as they can in as much detail as is available, firm in the belief that it could lead to something far greater. If that means starting at minimum wage...so what? Kerby and I started @ $0.85 per hour. I can't speak for Kerb, but for me? On day one I was overpaid!

The 'Formula' For Our Success

If such a formula exists here it is: Get noticed. Hire and train great people – and get 'the h' out of their way. Take your radio station (read: 'business') out of the studio (read: 'building') and into the community – literally. Keep things interesting and enjoyable for your listeners (read 'customers' or 'clients'). And where radio is concerned: when things are calm keep it *fun,* but when there's an emergency dedicate the station to providing information 24/7 until things get back to normal.

In *"WIGGLES, WINKS & WIZARDS: ..."* we'll describe, deal by sometimes-crazy deal, how we built our company from an AM/FM combo in Williamsport, PA to...well, you'll see.

Note: Our book also includes tales of incidental and perhaps 'off topic' events that occurred along the way. Some served to enhance business, others to enhance life. I hope you will find them interesting.

Last: I am deeply grateful for the privilege of working with so many great colleagues and for the excellent results they produced for our companies.

Without Kerby Confer as my partner none of this could have happened.

I hope you enjoy the story.

—Paul H. D. Rothfuss

CHAPTER 1
STEPPIN' AWAY

Nine AM, Friday, March 1, 1974.

The last few notes of Chuck Willis' "(I Don't Wanna) Hang Up My Rock And Roll Shoes" echoed in my head as I stepped out of the studio.

https://youtu.be/rcitG7FpMVg

Seventeen years of playing records and saying funny stuff was more fun than humans should be allowed to have...but it was over for me. On to the next!

I'd come to realize that my goal of owning a radio station would be unachievable unless and until I learned about the 'business end' of the radio business, aka radio ad sales. This was the deciding factor in my leaving the cushy confines of Metromedia and WCBM on Saturday, December 2, 1972 to take a fifty-percent pay cut; travel sixty-seven miles (pre-dawn) to Annapolis, MD to do the morning show on WYRE, attend a sales meeting, make sales calls through the afternoon and return to our home in Baltimore County; then arise at three AM next morning to do it all again.

I was going from a five hour 'working' day to a 12+hour *working day*...for half the money.

I understand why sane people would view such a move as illogical at best.

It was one of the two or three best decisions I ever made. (Marrying Barbie was Number One!)

Note: Each day I made the trip from Lower Beckleysville Road, Baltimore County, to Annapolis, toodling along in my red 'tomato can' - a 1967 Volkswagen Beetle, sans radio.

On day one I thought 'no radio' was a real pain. It would shortly be revealed to be one of the most significant unintended consequences I would ever encounter.

Four Shoes Hangin'

As we explained in "Alias Emperor Rodgers...," my long-time friend and 'business partner' Kerby Confer was the General Manager of WYRE.

In 1969 he hung up his R&R shoes for that opportunity, and along the way had earned a vested interest in the company that owned the station.

Says Kerb: "You'll join the staff at WYRE as the morning host. You'll do the morning show Monday thru Friday. You'll attend our sales meetings, learn radio sales and call on clients the rest of the day. If you make $100,000 in total ad sales your first year you'll come off the air and be named Sales Manager."

I saw this as a big opportunity...with (at last) weekends off.

I went 'all in'.

About WYRE

WYRE was a 'local' Annapolis radio station - a 250 watt daytime-only station located between Baltimore and Washington, DC. It was 'under the umbrella' of forty well-funded great-sounding radio stations, most with large 'footprints'.

One would think, *There's no way this station can succeed.*

One would be incorrect.

AM radio signals are enhanced when the station's ground system is laid out in wet ground, the water acting like a serious 'booster' of the station's 'ground wave' broadcast signal.

The WYRE tower was on a sort of swampy piece of ground located next to the Spa Creek. The ground system was in that field. The Spa Creek feeds directly into the Chesapeake Bay.

On dry land the primary coverage of a 250 watt AM station is a radius of about twelve miles, which to the west and northwest was the case with WYRE. However, to the north and south along the west shore of the Bay and across the water to the Eastern Shore, WYRE could be heard from Havre de Grace, MD to Occoquan, VA, fifty miles in each direction.

Realizing this, WYRE station ownership decided to provide specific programming that no metropolitan station would (or could) ever match. Sitting at 810 on the AM dial, the station became "Boat Radio Eight, WYRE - The Voice of the Bay."

WYRE Marine Weather
http://emperorrodgers.com/WYRE_weather.mp3

From April through October, the weekend population floating on and otherwise enjoying the Chesapeake Bay was equal to the population of Frederick, MD, the state's second-largest city.

WYRE broadcast Marine Accu-Weather, tide timetables, fishing reports, sailing club meetings, fishing derbies...basically all boating, fishing and/or *Bay-related* events were regular features of WYRE programming. Listenership doubled in these months.

The station had plenty of year-round local listeners and lots of traditional radio advertising clients. But it was the bonus market – the 'Bay-involved' added listeners that made the station a 'must' for advertisers desirous of reaching those masses of people enjoying the water and depending upon WYRE to provide them with great information. And of course, lots of Top Forty 'Hit Music'.

WYRE's twice-hourly Marine Weather Forecast sponsorships were sold out from April thru October.

At premium rates.

And...there was a waiting list!

First Day in Sales — Simply Marv-elous

Marvin Mirvis was a veteran Baltimore broadcaster, a master of the art of media sales and a fabulous businessman. He was the owner of WYRE.

It took about two minutes for me to learn that titles meant nothing to Marvin.

Marvin: "Titles on business cards are nothing more than legible ink smears. They don't matter. The only thing that matters is *what you do.*"

To Marvin, his name on the ownership documents of the radio station only mattered at the FCC, the IRS and his bank.

Monday thru Friday Marvin was a Media Sales Rep. He called on clients and made sales. Lots of clients and lots of sales.

He saved non-productive administrative stuff for weekends, most always away from the station. Lesson learned!

Up In The Morning And Out To School

Monday, December 4, 1972 - Nine AM. Training for my 'new career' began. I got off the air and reported to class - Professor Mirvis presiding.

MM - Lesson One: A Tale Of Two Stations

"Paul...Here's a story about two radio stations. Station One is located in a brand new studio and office facility. Equipment, furniture, spa...everything you could want is right there...all shiny and new. Staff members are well-educated, well-dressed and good-looking. The station sounds great.

"Sales are bad. Revenue is down. Station One has huge problems.

"Station Two is in a dilapidated double-wide that resembles a neglected chicken coop. Building's dirty - falling apart. Equipment and furniture is ancient and the front yard's a mess – a collection of rain-soaked magazines, assorted metal junk and an old cracked porcelain toilet.

"And weeds, Paul. Don't forget the weeds. Lots and lots of weeds. The staff is inexperienced and the men have bad haircuts. The station sounds like crap.

"Sales are great. Revenue is way up.

"Conclusion? Station Two has no problems.

"Moral? Great revenue cures all ills.

"Get it"?

"Yes sir."

MM Lesson Two

Marvin: "Every minute a salesman spends *not* in front of a client, he's unemployed. Need I say more"?

Honest to God, this is exactly how my sales training began.

The reality? It was the start of my 'someday I'm going to own a station' training.

But there's more. So much more.

MM Lesson Three

Marvin continued: "There are three things a radio salesman needs to know in order to be successful.

"One: He needs to know how radio advertising works.

"Two: It's even more important for him to know how his *client's* business works.

"Three: More important than #1 and #2 combined, he's gotta make a lot of sales calls. You can do simple math right"?

Paul: "Umm, yesss."

M: "So Paul, do you know how many calls it takes for a radio salesperson to sign a new client."

P: "Ummm, no."

M: "It takes an average of six calls. So for every client you sign at your first meeting there will be one who won't sign until you make your eleventh call, right"?

P: "Ahhh, that's a *lot* of calls."

M: "Right. O K. So...say I'm the world's best salesman and I close fifty percent of my calls but you're the worst...you close ten percent of yours. I make ten calls…you make sixty. You will make more sales than I will."

P: "Huh"?

M: "It's that simple. Ya gotta make a lotta calls. Get it"?

P: "Oh… Yeah. Got it. Lotta calls."

Marvin *(pointing his index finger):* "Riiight"!

I Get Ideas - MM Lesson Four

M: "Paul, can you operate a Dymo Labeler?"

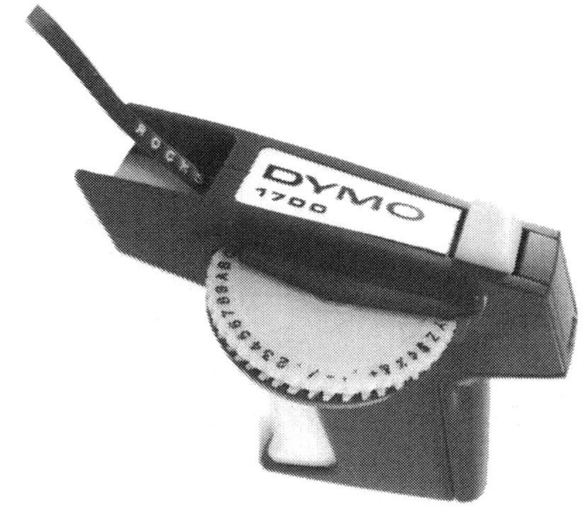

P: "Yes sir, I can."

M: "Good. Here *(handing the labeler to me)*. Type this."

I took the labeler. Marvin dictated and I selected the letters.

Ideas can be sold where merchandise can not.

When I'd finished I handed the labeler to Marvin. He clipped off the tape and handed it to me.

M: "Now - remove the backing and tape this to the back of your telephone handpiece. That way you'll see it many times every day.

"This is the key to our success."

Whaaat?

Never in my wildest dreams or craziest fantasies could I have conjured up where these lessons would lead. Most especially the *ideas* part.

You'll see.

Welcome to The Marvington Idea Factory

Marvin believed that we sold *ideas,* not *radio time*. WYRE was an idea factory.

Our sales meetings were more like brainstorming sessions. A salesperson would mention a client for whom they needed an idea and we'd brainstorm it 'til we came up with something. Ideas are what got us appointments.

Marvin: "Paul, here's how this works. You call a prospect and say, 'Mr. Jones, this is Paul Rodgers at WYRE. I have an idea for your business that I'd like to share with you. Can we get together Tuesday at ten o'clock?

"You'll be the *only* person calling him this week offering him *an idea for his business*. Other sellers will be drilling him for orders but *you* will be offering help for his business. This is the best way for you to get appointments and help you to make a lotta calls.

"Next, grab one of his newspaper ads or go to his place of business and walk around. Make notes about what you see. Then write and record a spec commercial, dub it onto a cassette, put the cassette in the recorder and go to the appointment."

What If I Don't Have An Idea

Marvin: "If you have no idea but lotsa guts you just put a blank cassette in the recorder and go.

"At the meeting make it obvious when you put the cassette player on the table. That way the cassette player becomes the subconscious focus of attention.

"Next, take out your tablet and your *Tell Me* form, and say, 'Mr. Jones, before discussing my idea may we talk for a few minutes? I'd like to learn more about you and your company.

"Ask him the questions on the *Tell Me* form, taking notes as he answers. This should take no more than ten minutes (*unless he wants to go on*), after which you say, 'Mr. Jones, I really thought I had a good idea here, but based on what you've told me I realize it's just the *germ* of an idea.

"Slowly picking up the cassette player you say, 'I need to go back to the station and work on this. May I have fifteen or twenty minutes with you on Monday, say, at eleven o'clock'?

"Via the *Tell Me* and your visit you'll have enough info to come up with a really good spec commercial, or even a theme for a campaign. Do that, then go back and make your presentation.

"Oh..and one more thing...when the spot finishes playing *say nothing*.

"He who speaks next, loses." (*grin)*

Note: 'Lesson Four' was the key that unlocked the magnificent success Kerby and I were to enjoy as we owned radio stations together (much more on this to come). For thirty years it was great ideas that enabled us to turn several handfuls of bad or underperforming radio stations into wildly successful stations.

Many became the top-rated stations in their markets. Over thirty years later many of 'our' stations still enjoy that status.

By Any Means Necessary

You can't make a sale unless you can see and talk with a potential client. At this, Marvin was a master. Also Marvin was a teacher...even when we wasn't teaching.

Check this out: I was at my desk one morning around nine o'clock when Marvin came in the office. He sat at his desk, picked up his phone and began to dial. (*You remember dial telephones, right?)*

What follows is the one-way conversation I heard.

"Hello John...it's Marvvvv. How are you today?

"Yes, I'm well thank you. Hey...I have a question for you. Do you have any stock for sale?

"No-no, I didn't mean the stuff you sell at your place of business - I mean stock in your company.

"That's disappointing. I was hoping I could buy some of your stock because I have an idea for you that's gonna make stuff fly outta your place. Do you have time to see me today?

"Great. I'll see you around two. Thanks, John."

Note: Marvin Mirvis was a brilliant man – one of the wisest, kindest most generous people I ever knew.

Marvin freely gave me all of his knowledge. He was a wonderful mentor and much loved.

A 'Top Gun' in my Mastermind Group.

I owe Marvin...big time.

CHAPTER 2
THE AD MAN

I attended my first sales meeting on Tuesday, Dec. 4, 1972. Right after the meeting Kerby told me he had something for me. I went to his office where he presented me with a brand new cassette player – "For you to use when presenting spec spots to clients."

This was cool…but there was more.

So much more.

Kerb also gave me a cassette recording called "The Strangest Secret."

"This is a copy of the first recording of the spoken word ever to sell one million copies. It's narrated by Earl Nightingale, a man who earns his living by going around the country giving lectures about achieving both personal and professional success. It's about forty minutes long.

"Give it a listen when you can. I think it will be helpful."

Helpful? It was a life-changer.

Skeptical Me

I thanked Kerby and took the recorder and cassette. The recorder needed no explanation – it made great sense to me.

As for the cassette, I couldn't fathom when I'd ever have forty minutes to sit and listen. Or how I'd be able to gin up the patience to do so.

Oh well.

You'll Never Get Him On

My very first sale served to cement forever my belief in the power of ideas. You won't believe this story.

December 4th is a lousy date to begin a media sales career. Retail businesses are the backbone of radio advertising but retailers are far too busy with Christmas business to see media people. Besides, most of their media buys have been in place for months.

At that first sales meeting Carl Monk (our Sales Manager) tore apart the *Annapolis Capital* newspaper, pulling out ads from those businesses that were not using our radio station.

He held up one ad after another and asked, "Who wants this one"? There were always plenty of volunteers.

"Who wants Eddie Leonard's"?

Crickets.

Silence.

"Who's Eddie Leonard," sez I.

"He's got a huge sporting goods store in Annapolis."

I raised my hand. "I'll take it."

Tee Hee

The sales staff snickered. "You'll never get him on. Everyone's tried. He doesn't like radio. It's too late for holiday business. Impossible." Etcetera, et cetera.

Ideas Can Be...

I looked at his ad and decided to visit the store.

They were right. The store was terrific and very well stocked…Annapolis' mecca for sporting goods...stuff for any sport imaginable.

Lost in thought, I walked around the store for five or ten minutes trying to come up with something that might suit his needs...or those of his customers.

There were more shoppers in the store than I would have imagined, especially for a Tuesday morning. And just twenty days before Christmas.

(Hmmm. Why are these folks here - and what are they looking for?)

And it hit me.

The holiday is coming fast. Most Christmas shopping is already done so these folks are probably last-minute shoppers looking for 'just one more' inexpensive gift that would be sure to please. Like a 'stocking gift'. Sooo…exactly what might that gift be?

I looked around some more…and realized that I was literally surrounded by the answer.

Balls!

Idea Time

I hurried back to the station where I wrote and produced the following thirty-second commercial:

> (b*asketball dribbles, sneakers squeak)* - "Hey baby! Ahm' an Eddie Leonard basketball. An' wid me…*(net swishes)*…it's nuttin' but net."

(Football contact sounds, gruff voice) - "I'm an Eddie Leonard Football. (*oof!) An' ya k*now what? I'm a touchdown machine." *(crowd roars).*

(Baseball crowd, bat hits ball, crowd cheers) – "I'm an Eddie Leonard baseball…a home run every time."

(*Golf crowd muttering - tee shot*) – [multiple voices} "We're a dozen Eddie Leonard golf balls gittin' ready for your first hole-in-one" *(ball lands in cup, crowd cheers).*

"If you're looking for a last-minute gift that's sure to please, head for Eddie Leonard's Sporting Goods in Annapolis.

"You'll have a ball…and on Christmas Day, so will someone you love."

I did all the voices. With editing and all it took about two hours to pull the spot together.

(*Red Alert: This was years before digital and multi-track recording. Broadcast veterans will fondly recall the old splicing block and razor blade 'technology'.)*

Comes Now the Contest

I patched the tape recorder into the phone line and called the store.

"May I please speak with Mr. Leonard"?

"Sorry, he's not in."

"When do you expect he'll be back"?

"Can't say. He's down in Easton, opening his new store."

"May I please have the phone number there"?

They gave me the number and I dialed.

Whoops!

"May I please speak with Mr. Leonard"?

"Just a minute."

Then, "Hello"?

"Hello, Eddie"?

"No, this is Larry. Eddie was my dad, but he passed away last year."

Ulp!

This is no lie. It's precisely how the conversation started. I was terribly embarrassed and wanted to hang up. I persevered.

"I'm sorry, sir. I didn't know. I apologize.

"I'm Paul Rodgers with WYRE radio. I realize this may be a bad time but I have an idea for your business."

"What is it"?

"I've created a thirty-second radio spot aimed at last-minute shoppers. May I play it for you"?

"Sure. Go ahead."

I hit the 'play' button and played the spot.

When it ended I pulled the patch cord. Marvin's words echoed in my brain.

("He who speaks next, loses.")

I sat silent, awaiting his reaction.

"That was very good."

"Thank you, sir."

"What'll it cost me to run it"?

"I can run twenty-four spots each week for the next two weeks for $380.00."

"Go with it. I'll be back in Annapolis tomorrow. Come see me."

I wanted to scream. Maybe I did, I can't recall.

Eddie Leonard's Sporting Goods was my first client…from my first-ever presentation.
You know…the guy no one could get on the station?

Except the *idea* could. And it did!

As scheduled, we met on Wednesday, December 6th. I took my cassette player and played the spot for Mr. Leonard again. He added a third week to the schedule.

We met again in January and I began to present him with a whole series of commercial ideas.

He advertised with us for the rest of 1973.

("Ideas can be sold where merchandise cannot.")

Can you say, "I'm a believer"?

A Fabulous Start

'Breaking its Maiden' is the descriptive terminology used when a Thoroughbred racehorse wins for the first time—in racetrack parlance, any Thoroughbred that has never won a race is referred to as a 'maiden'.

It is rare for a horse to 'break its maiden' in its first start. Maidens are most often entered in races that are for maidens only but occasionally, believing that his maiden might be of 'better stuff', a trainer will enter his horse to run in a high-level race, called a stakes race – a tough challenge to say the least.

I viewed my 'first call, first sale' experience as breaking my maiden in a stakes race. I was high as a kite for the rest of the day.

The 'Biggie Bell'

Mr. Mirvis believed that great news should always be shared with the entire staff.

He went to a nautical store and bought a Ships Bell which he bolted to the wall just outside the door of the sales office. Shiny brass it was, with a thin ten-inch leather strap tied to the clapper.

The entire staff was instructed to ring the bell..."whenever you have some *Really Big News* about WYRE."

Examples: The new ratings showed a nice increase in audience size. A staff member was celebrating the birth of a baby. A sales person had made a significant sale—whether for big dollars or not. The Marine Weather avails were sold out.

You get the idea.

Did I ring the bell? Hell...I was so excited I damn near tore it off the wall!

'No Radio' Meets 'The Strangest Secret'

Around four o'clock I cranked up the Volksy for the trip home. And whattheheck...with no radio on board I put 'The Strangest Secret' in the cassette player and hit 'Play'.

As I headed up 3/301 toward the Beltway and home, the magnificent bass voice of Earl Nightingale poured out of the speaker: "This is Earl Nightingale and I'd like to tell you about the strangest secret in the world."

Over the next several weeks Mr. Nightingale's message 'rode shotgun' for me. I listened to it in snippets nearly every day for several months.

He told and re-told me the story about the importance of goal orientation. His message fired me up! It changed my outlook and as a result, my life.

The Crux Of The Message

To Mr. Nightingale 'The Strangest Secret' is simple: "We become what we think about."

Roll that over your tongue a time or two. *We become what we think about.*

In listening to the message it became clear to me that I'd already been behaving exactly as recommended...without ever knowing that this was a behavior that can be *chosen* (indeed *should* be chosen) and implemented *at once.*

Which I did.

I could go on about this. Instead I highly recommend that you listen for yourself. The original narration is available on YouTube. Share it with friends and loved ones.

https://www.nightingale.com/strangest-secret-dvd.html

CHAPTER 3
UPS 'N DOWNS

My goal was $100,000.00 in sales in 1973, my first year. I missed it by $273.00.

A Nice Family Kind of Place

Ocean City, Maryland ("OC") is the playground for Baltimore/Washington. All roads from both metros run to the Chesapeake Bay Bridge at Annapolis.

Imagine the spring-summer-fall traffic from Thursday afternoon through Sunday evening, on a route that collects traffic from two major metropolitan areas and funnels it onto a long bridge with two lanes in each direction.

Imagine the Friday afternoon and Sunday afternoon multi-hour traffic jams.

Imagine the opportunity presented by this situation.

So, in February of 1974 a new 'fast food' opened in Annapolis.

Very nice facilities and really good food was the reputation enjoyed by English's Chicken and Steak Houses, a company with many locations lining the route from Annapolis to Ocean City.

One day at lunchtime I decided to give English's a try. Their food was great.

They weren't advertising with us which I found a bit offensive. I decided to try for an appointment.

(On my way back to the station I pictured the throng en route to marinas on Maryland's Eastern Shore and to OC...listening to WYRE...diggin' our music...loving the boating, fishing and weather info. Thousands of hungry folks just hoping that someone would reach out and guide them to great food...like right now! And I envisioned all those English's locations on the way to the shore.)

At the office I called English's and asked to speak with the person in charge of advertising.

"That would be Mr. Hermann, our President. May I ask who is calling?"

"Yes ma'am. I'm Paul Rodgers with WYRE radio."

"Just a moment."

When Mr. Hermann picked up the phone I identified myself as a Media Rep for WYRE radio in Annapolis, explaining that I had an idea for his business that I'd like to present to him.

At once Mr. Hermann began to express his disappointment with radio, but he did agree to give me an appointment. Then he asked, "Are you ever in Baltimore"?

"Yes, sir. Twice a week."

"I wonder if you could do me a favor"?

Mr. Hermann asked if I would stop by a Baltimore ad agency to pick up a tape of some spec commercials that the agency had produced for him. I said I'd be happy to do so and that I'd bring them when I came to see him the following week. He said he'd call the agency and let them know.

I had the appointment but now I needed an idea...and fast!

The Power Of A Jingle

At WYRE we had a vinyl-album library of customizable jingles called "The Producer" – jingles created by TM Productions in Dallas, Texas. I decided to listen to a bunch of them to see if anything fit.

After listening to four or five jingles I slipped the needle into the grooves of the TM jingle singers version of "It's A Nice Family Kind Of Place."

Fit? *This* was a giant Bingo!

I spent the next several hours writing scripts and recording them over the jingle bed, nine or ten spots in all, mostly sixties. I was happy with the spots. They sounded pretty good.

I dubbed them onto a cassette leaving about two seconds of dead air between the spots. This meant that once I pushed the 'Play' button Mr. Hermann would be hearing the jingle nine times in less than ten minutes.

I figured unless Mr. Hermann had a 'tin ear' he'd soon be singing the jingle himself.

Yechh!

A day or two later I stopped at the Baltimore ad agency to pick up the spots. They were on a reel and since I didn't know whether Mr. Hermann had a reel-to-reel recorder available I thought I'd better dub the spots to a cassette for him. This turned out to be more fortuitous than I could ever have imagined.

Note: This was all happening during the infamous gas shortages of 1973, which the agency had chosen to be the 'theme' or the 'idea' for their 'campaign'.

Back at WYRE I wound the reel on the tape recorder to listen to the spots…two of the most confusing commercial messages I'd ever heard. Simply awful they were.

Spot One: "We know there's a gas shortage and it's hard for you to drive around looking for stuff. English's Chicken and Steak House wants to help. If you have to drive more than three miles back and forth to English's we'll give you a ten-percent discount on your purchase. If your drive is from four to ten miles the English's discount will be fifteen percent, and if it's on the weekend the discount will be twenty percent. Just come in to English's and show us your driver's license. We'll calculate your driving distance, you'll have your discount and our great food."

Are you confused yet? I was...but spot two would prove to be much worse.

As it was playing I was envisioning folks in their cars...hearing this message while trying to calculate 'miles times discounts' in their heads...with nary a thought at all about English's Chicken and/or Steak.

These spots were awful – the worst. You had to be a math major to figure it all out.

Gas Lines Meet 'The Power Of A Jingle'

I decided to re-dub my cassette for the presentation. I put the two ad agency spots on first, then a five-second pause, then my nine or ten spots with about two seconds of dead air between the spots.

A few days later I drove from Annapolis 'daown the shuer' to Mr. Hermann's office.

I was excited about presenting "It's A Nice Family Kind Of Place." English's had no slogan at the time, and no coordinated ad campaign. I thought this one was perfect.

I put my cassette player on the conference table and handed Mr. Hermann the reel from the Baltimore agency.

"I thought you might want to hear the spots from the agency so I dubbed them to my cassette. May I play them for you"?

"Yes, Paul. Thank you."

I pushed 'Play'.

"Ten miles twenty percent, twenty miles thirty percent, twice each week twenty-five percent except Tuesday when…"

I watched as a look of disbelief washed over Mr. Hermann. He was slowly shaking his head and was about to speak when spot two began to play.

More of the same.

When spot two ended I pushed 'Stop' and sat quietly, awaiting his reaction.

What happened next nearly dropped me to the floor.

Mr. Hermann said, "This is a perfect example of why I'm so discouraged with radio. Can you believe that's the best they could do? Those spots are off target and confusing – just awful. I hated them. I just don't get it.

"All I want is something that says we're a *nice family kind of place*."

Right Hand Up To God. Those were his exact words.

For two or three seconds I sat in stunned silence…frozen in place.

Then, moving with the speed of a Slow Loris I pressed 'Play'.

The jingle singers started with "It's a Nice Place - a Family Kind of Place." Music under as I said, "English's Chicken and

Steak Houses." Singers back in with "It's A Nice Family Kind Of Place."

My recorded message filled the center of the 'donut' jingle, suggesting that folks travelling to and from the Shore for the weekend would find the trip much more enjoyable with the great food they'd find at English's Chicken and Steak House.

The singers returned with "It's a Nice, Family Kind of Place."

Eight or nine spots followed – in rapid succession.

(*By now he's gotta be humming this jingle.)*

The last spot ended with the singers - "It's a Nice, Family Kind of Place." I pushed 'Stop'...and waited for Mr. Hermann to speak.

And speak he did indeed!

"That's exactly what I want. It's perfect. When can we start? What kind of schedule do you recommend? Can I use these spots on other radio stations? What will the jingle cost"?

And again, "When can we start"?

Wings On My Feet

Mr. Hermann signed a 12-month contract with WYRE, to start at once.

I flew back to Annapolis (sans airplane) with a $24,000.00 annual contract in my briefcase.

Can Ideas Be Sold Where Merchandise Can Not?

You Bet'cha!

Note: This event was all the proof I'd ever need re the power of ideas and jingles. It would lead to great success for us as you will soon learn.

But'cha Can't Win 'Em All

Baldwin Tractor and Garden Supply was a large Annapolis business that advertised with our competition but refused to advertise on WYRE.

Like Eddie Leonard's Sporting Goods, everyone on the sales staff had tried to get them on – without success. Feeling my oats, I decided to give 'em a call.

Using my 'idea' approach I cold-called the business and asked for the owner, Mr. Frank Baldwin.

"Mr. Baldwin, this is Paul Rodgers with WYRE. I have an idea for your business that I'd like to discuss with you."

(I didn't. Have an idea, that is.)

"Can you see me on Thursday around ten AM"?

I got the appointment.

Cassette player in hand I showed up on Thursday, shook hands with Mr. Baldwin, took out my 'Tell Me' sheet and started asking questions.

I can't recall why, but our discussion soon turned to politics where Mr. Baldwin revealed the fact that he was a huge fan of Secretary of State Henry Kissinger.

At that moment an idea began to form. After a few minutes more (and sensing that I was about to be 'on too long') I decided it was time for me to make an exit.

I thanked Mr. Baldwin and, picking up my cassette player, told him that our discussion made me realize my idea was just a germ of an idea and I'd need some time to feather it out.

I told Mr. Baldwin I'd work on the idea and call him for another appointment.

I thanked him for his time and returned to the station.

The next day I wrote two sixty-second spots starring 'Henry Kissinger' in a phone conversation with Frank Baldwin. I played the part of Mr. Kissinger. Mr. Baldwin was...well...Mr. Baldwin.

I called Mr. Baldwin and explained my idea. He went for it like a duck on a June bug.

I went to his office, explained how we'd do this and dropped off the scripts.

Back at the station, I went into the studio and called Mr. Baldwin. With the phone line patched into our tape recorder I recorded 'Kissinger and Baldwin' having two sixty-second conversations all about spring gardening and how Baldwin Supply was 'the place' for folks to find whatever they might need.

(The spots turned out really good if I must say so myself. I was happy with them.)

I did a final edit of the spots, dubbed them to a cassette, and went back to Baldwin Supply where I played the spots for Mr. Baldwin.

He flipped out, using words like 'perfect' and 'sensational'.

("Got him" thought I.)

"These spots are great and I want my wife to hear 'em. May I have the cassette"?

"Of course," sez I, and absolutely certain that I would get a contract for adverting on WYRE I gave Mr. Baldwin the cassette.

"You Dirty Rat"
– James Cagney, 1937

The next morning, en route to WYRE, I dialed over to monitor the competition...where I heard Frank Baldwin in a phone conversation with Henry Kissinger.

The S.O.B. had taken the cassette to our competition to run on their station.

I was furious. Enraged. I stormed into the office and told Marvin what had happened.

Wisdom

Marvin sat quietly for a moment or two. Then he calmly said, "Well Paul, personal behavior is the only way one can truly measure another person's integrity. Obviously he has none.

"So go ahead. Take five minutes to be really angry. You can even storm around a little if you want to.

"Then pick up the phone book, go to the Yellow Pages and find five businesses that aren't currently advertising with us. Call them with 'an idea' and go get 'em on the air."

After a slight pause Marvin gleefully added, "It might be fun to find a competitor of Baldwin's and get *them* on with a great idea. That would help both *their* business and our business...but might just put a crimp in Baldwin's."

Grin.

Onward!

CHAPTER 4
HEADIN' FOR HOME

Important Note: In 1971 the Federal Government decreed that all car radios must have the capacity to receive both AM and FM stations. In the ensuing fifteen years this regulation would lead to the demise of AM radio as we had known it. In early 1975 neither Kerby nor I had given this one minute of thought.

In early 1975 Mr. Mirvis announced that he was selling WYRE. Kerb and I decided to try and buy the station.

There were several buyers in contention, bidding against one another and pushing the price far higher than we thought we should pay. We were disappointed but dropped out of the contest. By February 1975 Marvin had a signed contract.

We knew we'd be involuntarily out in a few short months.

No More Dreamin'

An early March afternoon found me in Kerb's office, discussing the upcoming sale of WYRE and how it would affect us.

Kerby: "Paul, we'll be out of here in a few months. What are we going to do"?

Me: "I don't know about you but I intend to be managing a radio station somewhere. But hey...why isn't 'now' a good time for us to buy our first station"?

"How would we do that"?

"We'd start by calling some brokers to find out what might be available."

We each grabbed a copy of *Broadcasting Magazine* and leafed to the back, to the *Classified* section featuring 'tombstone ads' for various brokers.

One such ad was for the Keith W. Horton Company. The listing showed them with an address in Elmira, NY and indicated that they '*specialized*' in representing small-market radio stations located primarily in the eastern US.

We dialed.

Mr. Horton answered.

We gulped!

Can you say 'We're New At This'?

We had no idea how to begin this conversation but we launched. It was definitely 'Fire! Ready! Aim!'

With Mr. Horton and his partner Dick Kozacko on the line, we introduced ourselves and proceeded to give them a brief outline of our broadcast experience and what it was we were looking to accomplish.

I distinctly remember breaking into a cold sweat when Mr. Horton turned the conversation to 'business' by asking the 'key' question.

"How much money do you have"?

Kerby and I looked at each other.

Ulp!

(What? You greenhorns thought you could make this call without being prepared to answer this question? Are you nuts?)

Truth is, we'd talked about this and concluded that if we sold our houses and pooled that money (along with every penny of 'other' equity we could lay our hands on) we *might* be able to come up with $150,000.00.

Note: It's important to remember that between us, Kerby and I had been in radio a combined thirty-five years. The most recent twelve years found us both working very good jobs with top companies. We each had equity in homes we'd owned for five to ten years, and we'd saved some money as well. No one would have called us 'wealthy' but we thought we just might be able to scrape together enough to get this ball rolling.

Ya Pays Yer Money 'an Ya Takes Yer Cherce

Messrs Horton and Kozacko must have believed that we could come up with the money because they started telling us about some of their listings...specifically, three opportunities that they thought might fit our budget and our goals.

We wrote down the information and told them we'd look it over and get back to them in twenty-four hours. Then we opened our reference material and dug in!

First Up...

...was a huge-footprint FM station – WAAL in Binghampton, NY, a 50kw Class B FM with antenna @ 500' above average terrain. This facility had huge potential having just switched its format to Rock.

We knew that WAAL (yes...it was called WAIL!) was en route to great success. But there was a problem. The station had great potential but no revenue. WAAL was 97% 'po' and 3% 'dough,' not enough dough to pay even one of us a salary of any kind."

Given that we'd have to put everything we had on the table we thought a 'zero-salary' situation was probably not a good way to start.

Oh, and one more thing. Each of us had three children.

We had to pass on this one.

Carry Me Back To Old Virginny

Next, they told us about an AM/FM combo in Charlottesville, VA, one of America's most beautiful towns in a gorgeous part of the country.

Now *this* one had possibilities. Having vacationed there a time or two, both Kerby and I loved the thought of pursuing this opportunity.

First thought? Go after it - full out.

Problem? The FM was a small-footprint station, a Class A - 3kw with antenna @ 300' above average terrain, not enough to cover the entire metro area. We adored the city and surrounding area, but because the market was so desirable (it's the home of the University of Virginia) it had attracted competition that was much better than that usually found in similar sized markets.

In addition, while there was *some* revenue it was not enough to justify even below-average salaries for both of us, beside which we couldn't envision any 'upside' that even came close to resembling that of WAAL.

We voted 'no'.

And Then: The Impossible!

It's good that we were sitting down when they told us about this one...an AM/FM combo in a small town in upstate Pennsylvania.

Williamsport, PA of all places. Our hometown!

WLYC-AM and WILQ-FM, nee WLYC-FM.

Some History

These two radio stations went on the air in 1947 when the FCC granted the licenses to Mr. John T. Keliher, owner of a very successful construction business in Williamsport.

Mr. Keliher was a good friend and frequent social guest in the home of Mr. and Mrs. James Love, my parents-in-law. Barbie and I were in the periphery of their company on several of these visits, and on at least one occasion (sometime in the mid-1960s) I casually asked Mr. Keliher if he'd consider selling the stations to me.

I assume he judged my question to be premature at best, probably wondering a). where I'd get the money, b). why I thought I could run the stations, and c). where in the hell I got the courage (*chutzpah?*) to ask the question in the first place.

If indeed this was his reaction...well...he was on solid ground.

Note: I recall a tiny nagging feeling of 'left-outedness' when late in 1972 I read in Broadcasting Magazine that Mr. Keliher had sold the stations. Thankfully that feeling quickly subsided and I totally forgot about it.

The Sequence

The FM was the first of the two stations to go on the air.

Originally WLYC-FM, the station was licensed as a Class B – 50kw @ 500' above average terrain.

An integral part of any FM license application is its proposed antenna location, in this case an ideal spot atop the Bald Eagle Mountain at its south-easternmost spot. From there the station broadcast with 9-kw @ eleven-hundred feet above average terrain, serving five central Pennsylvania counties with 60-db coverage.

This was a *very* large footprint radio station.

Note: In 1947 there were virtually no FM sets in use so the 'large footprint' made no difference at that time. No listeners, no revenue, right? 1975 saw more FM sets coming into use and the big 'Wham-O! was yet to come.

The grant of Mr. Keliher's AM license followed and WLYC-AM went on the air with 1-kw, daytime only. The AM ground system was co-located with the FM, but as great as this location was for FM signal enhancement it was twice-bad for an AM signal. Recall that AM radio signals are enhanced when located in wet ground. The mountaintop was high and dry 'rock on rock' for as far as the eye could see.

Ergo, the facility with the best chance to produce revenue – WLYC-*AM*, was located in the worst possible spot for signal enhancement, while WLYC-*FM*, with a near-zero chance of producing revenue was (as we would soon discover) 'sittin' in the catbird seat'.

The Details

Horton and Kozacko told us that the stations had produced revenue of $325,000.00 in 1974 and were on track for $375,000.00 in 1975.

According to *Broadcasting Magazine* the Williamsport 'market' had a total of $635,000.00 in radio ad revenue in 1974, up from $550,000.00 in 1973, meaning that WLYC and WILQ were garnering more than fifty percent of the ad dollars and were (probably) responsible for the momentum leading to an $85,000.00 year-over-year revenue increase.

Just two-plus years after being acquired these stations were performing exceedingly well. Surely there must be more upside, yet they were being offered for sale. We wondered why and were very curious to learn about the owner and what changes he might have made at the stations in those two years. We needed more information.

Asking price for the stations was $750,000.00, a price considerably higher than we could afford to pay. When we ran this past our lawyer - Jason L. Shrinsky, Esq. - he said, "If you pay a penny more than $550,000 for these stations you may have to get a new lawyer."

We told the broker we could not afford to pay that much for these or any stations.

They assured us that there was some 'wiggle room' in the asking price.

"Hi. We're The IRS, And We're Here To Help You"

A glimmer of hope appeared, emanating from the strangest place.

The IRS.

Seriously. A factor about which we could never have been aware.

Note: In 1975, IRS regulations stated that any seller perfecting an installment sale could, in the first year following the closing, receive a maximum of twenty-nine percent of the total sale price of the asset ...that if he chose to accept more than 29% he would be required to pay the total tax due on the entire transaction, the same as if he'd received all cash at closing.

"Oh," said Mr. Horton,"... and the seller is seeking an installment sale."

Billtown Or Bust

We viewed the stations as having a decent upside and lots of upward momentum...*and* they had enough revenue to pay each of us a mid-level salary. We chose to pursue this opportunity and asked the brokers to set up a meeting in Williamsport for a walk-thru and discussion with the Seller.

The Seller said, "Not without a signed Letter of Intent."

We had to make an offer.

Here Goes

We decided to offer the Seller $650,000, with 29% down ($188,500.00) and the remainder in installments paid over five years. (Shrinsky was apoplectic!)

We were turned down almost immediately.

Further conversation with the brokers revealed that one main reason for the 'no' was because the Seller was 'on the hook' for the five-percent brokerage commission ($32,500), which he would have to pay-in-full at closing. Doing so would leave him with just $156,000.00 in 'walk away' money, which he viewed as an inadequate amount in a deal of this size.

From this response Kerby and I thought he'd be a 'yes' if we came back with an offer of $682,500.00. (In other words, $650,000 + a $32,500 commission.)

But as we analyzed it further we came to the conclusion that the brokerage commission was *the* bugaboo standing in the way of our acquiring the stations - that he didn't want to pay a brokerage commission under any circumstances. Period.

We needed to find a way to get the commission 'removed' from the deal.

How to remove it?

Here's how.

"If Ya Could, Wouldja..."

We called the brokers and explained our rationale. They cited the fact that they were by contract entitled to the commission. We agreed.

Most importantly, they agreed with us - that the Seller viewed the commission as a major impediment, one that may be preventing this deal from getting done.

"So, Keith and Dick," sez Paul and Kerb. "What if *we* paid your commission"?

"What"?

"We'll pay your commission if you'll agree to take the payment in installments, with us as the payer. Will you do that?"

To our great surprise and joy, Messrs Horton and Kozacko agreed.

(*We had no idea how charming we were!)*

We went back to the Seller with the following offer: A purchase price of $617,500.00 for the assets; $167,500 down with the remainder in a five-year note, payments of principal and interest (@ 7%) to be made monthly. And *we* will pay the brokerage commission.

Note: The seller never asked how we intended to pay the commission and we never told him.

The answer was an immediate 'yes'.

(Shrinsky was apoplectic – "You're paying too much." Thankfully he stayed with us and was our FCC Counsel for many years. He is a wonderful friend as well.)

Kerby and I agonized over the fact that the stations were located in Williamsport, PA. True, it was our hometown, but we hadn't lived there for fifteen years. In considering whether to pursue this deal, not knowing how we'd be greeted upon returning was firmly on the 'minus' side of our 'plus/minus' list. In reality, it turned out to be somewhat of a plus. Soon after the announcement of our acquisition of the stations a rumor began circulating in town. 'Those guys got their money from the mafia.' Go figure!

The lesson? It's not always <u>how much</u> you pay for an asset. Sometimes it's <u>how you pay for it</u>. This lesson soon proved to be of immense help to Kerby and me. You'll see.

We formed our new corporation – Pennsylvania Radio, Inc. - and it was on to the closing.

More About The Seller

The Seller was Alpha Broadcasting, Inc., owned by Mr. George Vajda (pronounced VOY'-da), a true American success story and a certified character. George once sent me a nasty letter threatening to call our note.

He signed it, *"Cordially, George."*

Mr. Vajda was also President of Alpha Computer Company which came into existence in the early fifties when computers were the 'next big thing'.

Short version: Companies of all sizes wanted to own computers but couldn't afford to buy them. Mr. Vajda and a partner bought a computer (which in those days were room-sized) and began leasing usage-time to some of the aforementioned companies.

Demand soon exceeded supply so they bought another computer, then another. And so forth. Before long they were both wealthy men.

George Vajda was wildly intelligent and very cagey. As I recall he was a native of Hungary and a Naturalized American citizen. How he got interested in radio station ownership I do not know.

Thank You X 1000

Our first acquisition was made possible by the following important factors:

In the 1950s Mr. Galen D. Castlebury gave a couple of teenagers the opportunity to get into radio broadcasting. The minimum wage law, $0.85 per hour in 1958, made *his* risk minimal.

It made *our* opportunity possible.

These two young men discovered they had a 'knack' for radio and they came to love the industry. Over time their great success (both on and off the air) provided them with the credibility they needed to pursue radio station ownership.

The brokers of the Keith Horton Company (Keith Horton and Dick Kozacko) took a chance on these two young broadcasters, whom they hardly knew.

A Seller (Mr. George Vajda) felt comfortable enough with these two young men to take back a $450,000 note, holding the assets of the radio stations as collateral.

IRS regulations favorably aligned with Seller's needs and the Buyer's ability to pay.

Many thanks to all these people.

And the IRS!

Final Note Re WYRE

Are you kidding?

Can you imagine the disaster that would have befallen us had we taken everything we had and rolled the dice on a 250-watt *daytime only* radio station...under the umbrella of *fifty* viable Baltimore/Washington stations where 'just the other day' (prior to the energization of thirty FM stations *now presenting programming in stereo*) there were less than twenty stations that mattered?

As it turned out the new owners of WYRE enjoyed a few years of success before the added competition from the now-*killer* FM stations made the competitive landscape untenable.

No doubt you are aware of the old adage, "Be careful what you wish for because you might get it." Yes, it was disappointing at the time. But while we loved living in Maryland, our failed attempt to purchase WYRE was one of the best things that ever happened 'for' us. I have no doubt - it saved us from bankruptcy.

A Remarkable Partnership

Our partnership grew from a friendship that began when Kerby and I were thirteen and performing in a Christmas play at Thaddeus Stevens Jr. High School in Williamsport, PA.

In those first years we worked for other companies and later for *our* companies.

Thirty years together. No documents. Just a handshake.

More laughs to follow!

CHAPTER 5
G'BYES, CRICKETS AND WOODEN SHOES

The closing date for the purchase of WILQ/WLYC was set for August 1, 1975 in Williamsport. We had lots to do before that date.

First, in mid-May Kerby and I informed Marvin about our purchase of the stations. We listed our houses for sale and I said goodbyes to my pals at WYRE on June 1.

Next on my list was an early June visit and conversation with my Dad who, at age eighty-two, was in University Hospital in Baltimore awaiting another surgery on a hip that he'd broken in 1968. (*On a far more serious note Dad was also battling bladder cancer.*)

I told Dad that we'd signed the contracts to purchase the radio stations. He was excited about that news. I also assured him that as soon as possible after the closing I'd come to Baltimore and bring him back home to Williamsport.

He was *really* excited about that.

Community Ascertainment

Part of the FCC Application for Transfer of Control of the stations was a requirement that the buyer conduct personal interviews with upwards of thirty community leaders. This was meant to assure the FCC that the buyer was cognizant of the major needs of the community and would be able to present Public Affairs programming aimed at those needs.

I headed to Williamsport and attacked this project diligently, interviewing the Mayor, County Commissioners, Pastors, Rabbi's,

Priests, the DA, the Police Chief, business leaders, etc., etc., furiously taking notes that would be turned into individually typed reports that would become a file of over 100 pages.

Keep in mind – I was not acquainted with any of these folks before these meetings.

Sidebar: I doubt if anyone at the FCC ever read even one page of this, let alone the entire report. My evidence follows.

Wax On, Wax Off

Without a doubt, the most interesting and surprising interview I conducted was at the office of Mr. Clive Waxman, Director of the Williamsport Hospital.

(*If only I'd known...*)

We met and exchanged pleasantries, after which I explained the purpose of the meeting and the interview, which was to take about fifteen minutes.

I asked Mr. Waxman all the obligatory questions: Are there medical needs in the community that are being unmet, how is the economy here, do you have problems recruiting good staff...and on and on. He seemed to be very sincere with his answers. I was pleased.

For each interview I saved my *coup de grace* question for last.

Looking him right in the eye and using the most earnest tone I could muster, I said, "Mr. Waxman, what is the single most important thing that this community needs"?

He leaned forward on his desk, fixed me with a stare and said, "What Williamsport *really* needs is a damn good whore house."

And he wasn't laughing.

I froze.

He said, "You're not writing. Start writing. I need you to write that down."

Oh...ahmmm...no. You must be joking, I stammered.

"Not joking. Not at all. Please. Write that down. I mean it. We *really* need one."

It was hard for me to stifle a laugh but he had me convinced. Dutifully I wrote down what he said and asked that he initial my notes. We made some small talk and I went on my way.

I included Waxman's 'Needs Analysis' in my ascertainment notes, which were attached to the application and sent to the FCC.

I was absolutely horrified the day the FCC called to grill me about my community ascerta.... Oh, wait.

From the FCC? Crickets! Told ya so!

Note: By chance we'd purchased a home in Williamsport just a few doors up from Waxman's home. I soon learned that Clive was a great neighbor...and a certified wild man.

The Closing

We closed on the radio stations on August 1, 1975. Jason L. Shrinsky, Esq. represented us. Mr. Vajda represented himself.

The closing went off without a hitch.

As Kerby and I were leaving George came over to us and said (with his distinctive Hungarian accent), "You boys vill do well vit tese stations.

"I got tzem down (the competition).

Now...You Kick Them!"

A few days after the closing we received this in a letter from George:

> *With respect to your question as to the future potential of WLYC/WILQ-FM; the following is my opinion:*
>
> *Provided, that a new owner maintains or improves the quality of programming and a steady promotion policy, the two stations can easily double their income within 3 years and improve it even after that.*

He went on to explain his rationale for such a bold prediction. In fact, we were fortunate to be able to exceed his predictions ... by a lot ... and ours as well.

Some History

When George bought the stations in 1972, with the exception of WMPT (the Top Forty station that went on the air in 1958 where Kerby and I began our careers), programming on the rest of Williamsport stations had been largely unchanged for decades, and all of the FM stations were just simulcasting their AM programming.

In 1973 George changed the WLYC format to Top Forty. For WILQ-FM the format became Country during the day, then at sundown - WLYC sign-off time - WILQ picked up the Top Forty format where WLYC left off.

In essence this was an FM Country 'daytimer' and an AM/FM 'combo Top Forty.

Awkward, yes...but *very* clever; and more importantly...successful.

George also hired talented young DJ's from State College, PA - Penn State grads who'd been 'interning' at the local stations there. They were the epicenter of the talented staff we acquired at that closing. And he employed Croy Pitzer as his program consultant. Croy was a long-time broadcaster and free-lance performer in State College, PA and had brilliantly tutored many of the young DJ's referred to above.

There can be no doubt: To that date and time Croy Pitzer was the most talented broadcaster that had ever appeared in Williamsport. He had these babies humming!

When George bought the stations (1972) their gross annual revenue was less than $75,000.00 vs total market revenue of approximately $350,000.00. When we closed they were on-track to produce $375,000.00 in 1975.

George did indeed 'get them down'.

And yes – we were about to kick 'em. I mean *really* kick 'em.

Hard.

Pennsylvania Radio, Inc.

We named our corporation "Pennsylvania Radio, Inc." Kerby designed our very cool logo.

At the suggestion of business lawyer (and friend) Marvin H. Schein, Esq., Kerby and I each purchased our stock for $17,500.00. The remainder of our money went into the company as loans.

We're in business!

Marvin and Kerby met in 1971 or '72 while standing in a line at the Charles Theatre in Baltimore, waiting to see Tom Jones. Kerby needed a lawyer to handle some business affairs.

They instantly liked one another and Marvin was hired. They'd worked together for a couple of years so it was logical that we'd choose Marvin to represent our young broadcasting company.

Marvin's 'hobby' was playing a magician – 'Shazmo The Great.' Can you imagine the sparks that fly when a magician meets a couple of disc jockeys? Marvin was also a CPA. More on Mr. Schein to follow.

Dr. Paul A. Rothfuss

In early July, several weeks before the scheduled August first closing, I visited Dad at the senior care center in Catonsville, MD where he was residing following the hip surgery. I told him of my plan to go to Williamsport in the next few days to prepare for the closing and get squared away in the new business...and that sometime during the week of August 10th I'd be back in Baltimore to pick him up and 'bring him home'.

I also told him I'd probably be out of touch for a few weeks but not to worry: my brother David (who also lived in Baltimore) would be in to see him in the meantime.

Dad said he understood.

Note: In spite of his rapidly declining physical health my father never lost one scintilla of his intellect. His mind was always razor sharp and his memory keen.

So... I was off to Billtown and 'on to the next'.

We closed on the stations and I spent the first ten days getting to know our new staff and 'learning where the envelopes were stored'.

Wooden Shoes

By Monday, August 11th I was pretty much up to speed, so it was time to call Dad and set up his trip back home.,I called the center and asked to speak with Dr. Rothfuss. They rang Dad's room.

Dad answered with his always-mellifluous tone: "Hellooo."

"Hi Dad, it's...'

He cut me off with..."Well where in the hell have YOU been. I hadn't heard from you in so long I was about ready to send out for a pair of wooden shoes."

(Oh no, I thought. I can't believe this. Dad's lost it.)

Hesitatingly I said, "Wooden shoes? Why would you need wooden shoes"?

"Because I was going to kick your ass next time I saw you. Don't you *ever* go three weeks without calling me, do you understand"?

Nothing new here. This was my Dad at his very best. He hadn't 'lost it' at all. Fact was, he was as keen as ever.

I offered apologies and explained that I'd be down Thursday or Friday to bring him home.

“That will be wonderful son. Thank you. I can't wait to see you.”

“I love you Dad. See you Thursday or Friday.”

“I love you too.”

Other Plans

Wednesday morning, August 13, 1975 around 6:30 my phone rang. It was Mrs. Peterman, the director at the center.

“Paul, your Dad died early this morning.”

The Wooden Shoes conversation was the last I would have with my Dad.

God had other plans…

…and Dad was finally home.

Note: Dr. Paul Arndt Rothfuss was a very fine man and a top-notch Blue Ribbon Award-Winning father. My first and most influential mentor. I think about him nearly every day. When stuff happens or during certain conversations I know exactly what he'd say and exactly how it would sound. I think I should write a book about my Dad. I'll call it “THE DEAR DOCTOR.”

CHAPTER 6
OPPORTUNITY WITH A CAPITAL 'O'

Pennsylvania Radio, Inc. opened for business with yours truly at the helm. Kerby was in the process of helping Marvin get WYRE to its closing and would be joining me in mid-September.

Prior to the start I had no idea about what to expect. However, any expectations I may have brought on board would have paled at the reality of what unfolded.

Serendipity x 1000!

One of the first things I did was get a Biggie Bell and hang it in the Sales Office.

For Openers...

We asked the former General Manager to stay on for a few days after the closing. I thought it a good idea to have him on hand to show me around. I walked through the offices, introducing myself to the staff – shaking hands with everyone and thanking them for being on board.

Next came a meeting with the former GM. I wanted to get his take on 'who was what and who' on the staff.

You Can't Make This Up

"So, let's talk about the staff," sez I.

"OK Paul, but here's the first thing you need to know," he said. "You must always be vigilant – watch the employees like a hawk.

"Remember this: The employee will f**k you at every turn."

I couldn't believe what I'd just heard. I was shocked.

Perhaps I'd been spoiled by working with true professionals in companies like Susquehanna and Metro Media, but *this* comment was far, far away from my natural way of thinking.

I was speechless.

(If this attitude is what emanates from the top of this organization the staff must hate this guy. Achieving this level of success with this kind of leadership? This must be one helluva staff!)

Wait. It gets better.

Next question: "So who is the best person on your air staff"?

"Jim Cameron," he said.

"Is he the Program Director"?

"No. He's the all-night guy on WILQ"

(*Whaaaat?)*

"Ohhh Kaaay... sooo...your best guy is doing overnights, right? Why"?

"Geez...Do you know how hard it is to find someone who'll work an all-night shift *anywhere*"?

On hearing this I wanted to dash around the building yelling 'Huzzah!' while tossing rose petals in the air. (Sadly I was without rose petals.)

After that I ended the meeting. I figured I'd be better off learning about our colleagues on my own and with no further input from anyone.

I called Kerby and told him the good news.

(*This opportunity is far better than we thought.*)

Staff

Here are the folks Kerby and I inherited. I hope I can remember everyone. Apologies to those I may omit.

Note: Very quickly it became evident that this was a group of enthusiastic people who liked radio but who were a bit 'on edge', somewhat fearful about 'the new owners'. A natural reaction, right? They'd been waiting for 'real radio guys' to appear and participate with them – side-by-side. They had goals...and they wanted to learn what they needed to do in order to achieve them.

Here we go:

Colleen McCarty was our upbeat receptionist. When Colleen answered the phone, her melodic "WILQ/WLYC...How can I help you" made callers feel at ease.

Marie Kehler and Pat Mraz comprised our Traffic Department, two intelligent hard-working young women that we quickly learned we could count on.

John Ellis was our Chief Engineer. Also a helluva big band and jazz drummer. John a.k.a. "Snake" was as good as it gets. (More on the nickname to follow.)

Our sales staff consisted of four women and one man. Ruth Reeder, Cecelia "Cecil" Hook, Dave Banks, Linda White and Donna McQuillen.

Champions all.

Ruth Reeder was a sweet lady who loved her job. Ruth knew just about everyone in the area and never *ever* missed her monthly sales goals. Her clients *loved* her.

Note: Ruth retired in 1981. We had a retirement party at the Oaks Club and I presented her with a necklace – a pretty gold chain with an engraved gold Biggie Bell (a teeny bit larger than a thimble). I hated that she was leaving our company.

Cecelia Hook ('Cecil') grew up in Mt. Carmel, PA, some fifty miles south of Williamsport. Cecil had one rule: Call on everyone - often.

Here's a 'Cecil Story': One late afternoon while driving back to the station she passed a strip mall where she noticed a dim light inside a store that had been vacant for nearly a year. She swung into the parking lot, got out of her car and went to the door which, surprisingly, was unlocked.

Stepping just inside the door she said, "Hello...anyone here"?

A gentleman emerged from the back of the building. "May I help you"?

Cecil introduced herself and handed the man her card.

"WILQ? Great. I was hoping to get in touch with someone from your station."

Turned out that his company was about to open two supermarkets in the area and he wanted to be sure his advertising was in place prior to the opening. A few days later Cecil signed him to a sizable annual contract.

Over the years I worked with many outstanding sales colleagues, none better than Cecil. As a tribute to Cecil's always 'powerful' performance Jim Cameron referred to her as 'Cecil the Diesel'.

For us **Dave Banks** was 'The Lone Ranger' – the only male on our sales staff and one of the most ambitious and creative people I've ever known. He took to our 'idea sell' faster than a ten-year-old takes to ice cream.

Dave was a man of great courage. He handled the account of a client who was impossible to please. IM-POSSIBLE! This guy cancelled his account more often than he brushed his teeth, most often for no measurable reason. He was a real nut case!

But guess what? Where most salespeople would have thrown their hands up in desperation Dave stayed the course.

And he *always* got him back on the air. Every...single...time. Usually at a higher rate!

Brilliant!

Dave was a natural entrepreneur and eventually a station owner.

Linda White was in her twenties, but as a media rep she was wise beyond her years.

Linda handled our biggest account, Jack Lowry Dodge. From the teeny tiny town of Jersey Shore, PA 'The Good Guy In The White Hat' was the third largest Dodge dealer in America. Early on Linda took me to meet Jack.

His ad campaign, 'The Detroit Connection', was created by the Leon Shaffer Golnick Agency in Baltimore. "You're Headed In The Right Direction When You Get It...Right From The Detroit Connection."

Because we have a pigeon at the plant we get 'em for less...so we can sell 'em for less. Get it?

During my first month Linda took me up to meet Jack.

Following the obligatory 'hellos' I said to Jack, "So how do you like your ad campaign"?

Jack fired back. "What difference does it make? I could be 'The Good Guy In The White Hat' or 'The Rottenest SOB In Pennsylvania'...but if I advertised on 56 radio stations – which I do – I'd still sell the same number of cars."

Jack blanketed the twin tiers of PA and NY with his ads – using stations from Hornell to Waverly, NY and from State College to Tunkhannock, PA.

Wearing his white cowboy hat, Jack appeared in parades all over the region sitting proudly on the back of a beautiful Tennessee Walking Horse – an Appaloosa no less. What a guy!

I enjoyed Linda's candor. There was never a doubt about where she stood.

Donna McQuillen was the youngest person on the staff. She was a 'newbie' when we arrived but quickly proved her mettle via attention to detail and making her monthly quotas. I thought she'd be a terrific media rep, which she was.

Note: For that day and time this was a highly unusual 'balance' as most radio stations employed very few women in sales.

The Lesson: I soon learned that women bring a specific strength to sales positions that many men do not possess. Women tend to be better listeners and therefore are better 'tuned' to pick up on exactly what a potential client is seeking. I haven't checked lately but I'd bet today's media sales departments feature more women than men. Just sayin'.

Get Tied On

Our group of five professional media reps was already doing a fine job. Unknowingly, we were all on the verge of a rocket ride.

As a first-time owner/operator this was my first sales staff - 'The First Five'. As I look back on these fine folks I've often thought how great it would have been if I could have cloned them, and on 'day-one' installed the clones at every station we would eventually buy. Wow!

Over the next six years we were privileged to work with many fine media reps, among them: Curt Van Loon, Barb Cameron, Mike Steinhilper, Warren Diggins, Chris Pellegrino, Greg Adair, Fred Garrett, John Quinn, Gail Tuomisto, Bob Jackson, Don Steese, and on and on.

I know I've missed some folks here.

Apologies.

Three Stations in Two?

Recall that WLYC-AM was in a Top Forty format. A 'daytimer', it was on the air only from sunup to sundown.

The WLYC air staff: Lou Kolb, AM Drive, Barry Drake, PD and mid-days, Ted Genevish, PM Drive.

WILQ was in a Country Music format but changed to Top Forty when WLYC signed off the air. Cumbersome? Yes, but for a while, very effective.

On WILQ: Joe Dalto, AM Drive, Jim Cameron and Gary Jacobs, mid-days, Bill Wilson, PM Drive, Vince Grande, overnights.

Rick Andree did Top Forty from seven to midnight.

Lori Shannon was the news director and Lee Troisi did sports.

At no time, in all the stations Kerby and I owned, did we have a more dedicated, motivated, or talented staff.

Note: FM was in the very early stages of viability and AM was still king. But this was changing rapidly.

To many observers the Country Music format made no sense. Not for Williamsport and not for FM. We never asked George Vajda why he'd chosen the format for 'the Q'.

We were just a few months away from learning what a great decision this was.

Such Talent

Over the next several years many talented people joined the staffs of WILQ/WLYC, many of whom went on to accomplish great things.

Just to mention a few:

Peter Drew – A leading free-lance voice in Boston.

Bruce McDiarmid (Mac McCoy, WILQ) – As he used to say, "From Australia – the land of kangaridginees and abaroos." Mac returned to Queensland where he enjoyed great success on radio and TV.

Frank Bell (WLYC PD) – Now an executive with the Taylor Swift organization.

Vanessa Hunter (C & Q News Director) – Billtown native; Penn State grad; award-winning broadcaster. One of Pennsylvania's most respected news reporters.

Bill Keen (Sports Director) – No Bill, No Sports Presence. It's that simple.

Brad Nason (News) – Now an Associate Professor/Media Arts at Penn College.

Lou Kolb (WLYC) – Talented. Much loved. A true 'pro'. Lou retired from his on-air show in August, 2019. He will be missed.

Don Steese – A Susquehanna Valley legend.

Mark Lindow became a terrific Program Director at several stations; Paul Cavanaugh joined us from Annapolis and was a great 'Morning Host' on WILQ; Russ Ryan had a huge career as PD, a GM et al, in some of America's most important markets; Hugh Finn was a budding star as a TV 'weather guy'. His life was cut short in an automobile accident in Louisville, KY; Larry Miles, now knockin' 'em dead in the real estate business; Myra Sterner, a talented news reporter who was unwittingly a part of my 'Life's Most Embarrassing Moment' (more on that to follow); Judy Goldy, copywriter extraordinaire. And Diana Frank, Doug Herendeen, Paul Herbert, Jack Richards, Jill Uskurait, Dave Wollet...so many excellent and talented folks.

I know there are people that I missed. Please accept my sincere apologies.

Strip Marketing

Recall: In ALIAS EMPEROR RODGERS we talked about Susquehanna Broadcasting and how they 'renamed' the coverage area of their stations to reflect something larger than just their city of license.

On WARM, rather than saying 'WARM – Scranton, Wilkes-Barre' it was 'Warm Land.' WSBA used 'WSBA-Land' rather than 'WSBA – York, Lancaster, Harrisburg.'

We chose 'The Susquehanna Valley' for our reference point - on-air, in advertising, on print pieces and promotions, etc. And a jingle.

"W I L Q-----Sus.que.han.na Valley" which became a major element as we imaged the stations as 'regional' instead of 'local'.

Ramping It Up

Before the closing we signed two contracts that proved to be key to the sensational growth that followed. Both contracts granted us exclusive radio-broadcast rights to their services for seven counties in North-Central Pennsylvania: Clinton, Columbia, Lycoming, Montour, Northumberland, Sullivan, and Union. In other words, all the counties within the footprint of WILQ.

One was an agreement with Dr. Joel Myers' Accu-Weather. Accu-Weather gave us instant credibility in the local business community, plus sponsored Accu-Weather forecasts generated substantial revenue for us.

The other was a contract with TM Productions for 'The Producer' (customizable jingles) as well as an extensive library of musical beds and sound effects for producing our own commercials.

The TM products and the training Kerby and I would provide gave our sales staff the opportunity to ask for (and often get) larger percentages of the advertisers' advertising budgets.

Why?

Because a major 'secret' to success via radio advertising is consistency of message. Nothing delivers that better than a jingle.

Want some proof? O K. How many jingles can *you* sing?

"You Deserve A Break Today, So Get Up And Get Away to…"

'And like a good neighbor…' (*Riight. It's State Farm. I caughtcha!*)

"We are Farmers. Bum bad-um bum bum bum bum!"

How about an oldie but goodie. "See the U S A in your…"

The sales staff had been trained to sell advertising in bulk annual packages, a new concept for us. We soon learned how our method of selling jingles fit this concept perfectly.

Did it ever. And away we went.

An AIR-2 Genie Rocket

When we took over the stations on August first they were on track to hit $375,000.00 total revenue for 1975.

At our first August sales meeting I introduced the concept of selling ideas to our sales staff. This was easy. I simply repeated the lessons I'd learned from Marvin Mirvis and told them a couple of my personal stories. (See Chapter One.)

"So…where will these ideas come from?" they asked.

"Ten days from now you'll forget you ever asked that question. I promise."

Under the guise of 'meeting the new owner' I had each sales person take me on a sales call or two, during which the two of us would walk around the clients' place of business and I'd point out things that might be idea starters. Pretty soon *they* were doing this themselves.

"A key starting point is discovering the advertiser's 'U S P' – his Unique Selling Proposition. In other words, what is it that they do or have that is unique to their business, that no other competitor has or can claim.

"Maybe they're the only auto dealership that has purple ceilings in their building. If that's their U S P you create an ad campaign around that fact. I'm serious.

Could be they're in a rather remote location: *We know we're kinda off the beaten track but when you compare our prices we know you'll be back. Besides, who doesn't enjoy a nice drive in the country.*

I gave them blank copies of our "Tell Me" survey (now referred to as a 'Client Needs Analysis) and showed them how to use it.

"Always end the client meeting with a 'Tell Me' – you are interviewing the prospect about their business, writing down what they say."

One of the questions was: "So tell me. What is your Unique Selling Proposition – your U S P. What is it that you have or you do that no one else does"? Strangely, many business people had difficulty answering this one.

"In our sales meetings we'll spend time brainstorming, where anyone needing a client idea can share info about the business and the 'assembled multitude' can kick it around until we come up with something."

Very early on we started closing quite a few new accounts, a good sign.

Note: During our first six weeks Kerby got to spend a few days with us from time to time. If as individuals Kerby and I had energy levels of, say, 9 (total:18), when we worked together the total was at least 55!

By the time Kerby joined us 'full time' around mid-September we were already showing signs of serious growth. Two weeks after his arrival, with two of us there, going on sales calls, helping with ideas, writing and producing great spec spots and commercials, teaching the 'idea' sell and how to sell jingles, etc., etc., the lid was lifting off the kettle.

By October first we realized we had a chance to add an additional $50,000.00 to our projected 1975 revenue and end the year at $425,000.00 total gross revenue.

Bob Marley, Where Are You

Kerby and I shared a 12' x 12' 'executive office'. The fronts of our desks were pressed together, the desks and our chairs being the only furniture in the room. This was a great atmosphere in which to develop plans!

So what kind of incentive can we offer the sales staff if they hit four twenty-five? We made the announcement at the sales meeting the next day.

"OK guys, here's the deal. We have a great chance to finish the year with combined revenue (Alpha's plus ours) of $425,000.00.

"On September 30 we're at $325,000.00. If we can produce $100,000.00 in the final three months we'll hit that number. If we do, in February you and your significant other will join us for a long weekend in Jamaica."

They were absolutely astonished. Flabbergasted even.

Why?

Two reasons: One, this was the first time anyone ever 'revealed' station revenue to them, and two, they'd never before been offered a meaningful incentive. Did our plan work?

Next morning we walked into the sales office to find a 'map' leading from Williamsport to Jamaica.

Someone had taken several rolls of substantial glossy paper (about 12-inches wide), carefully unrolled it and stapled it to the top of the dry wall around the entire office – like crown molding. Drawn on the paper were cities, states and the ocean we'd fly over en route to Jamaica. Williamsport was 'start' and Jamaica was 'finish'. Along the 'route', wrapped around the heads of several pins, was a string of monofilament fishing line on which at 'Start' hung a 2 x 3 inch toy plastic airplane.

The map also contained revenue growth numbers in ten thousand dollar increments spaced nicely along the map, the tenth of which was located...you guessed it...in Jamaica.

(10 x $10,000 = $100,000, right?)

Kerb and I were knocked out by this show of spirit. What a buy-in, and this after just two months. Why, they hardly knew us.

We were pumped!

At our meeting that morning the staff decided we should move the airplane once each week and that the salesperson who added the most revenue or landed the toughest new client would get to move the plane.

Short Version

By December 5th we'd overflown Jamaica en route to…Cartagena, Colombia? I dunno. Anyway, we ended 1975 with combined revenue of $437,000.00. The sales staff was so hot I was afraid they'd melt the Biggie Bell.

Jamaica was great! Especially compared to North-Central Pennsylvania in February!

'The Group' arrived in Ocho Rios on a Friday morning – five salespeople and significant others plus Barbie and me. We taxied to a really nice hotel, put our stuff away and wasted no time getting to the beach.

Over the next three days some folks took a tour or two, but most of us hung out at the hotel and the beach enjoying the ocean and the sun and the Piña Coladas! Ahh, the Piña Colladas. And the food was great too! I think it safe to say a good time was had by all.

We arrived back in Williamsport with an energized sales staff…

…and an AIR-2 Genie rocket of a sales team on our hands.

The Culprit

My recollection is that the map was Dave Banks' idea.

'Creative' can't come close to describing Dave. Genius maybe? How about 'Creative Genius'?

Perfect!

Precis'

So...we'd sold our homes in Crofton, pooling every cent we had (and some we didn't have) and bought WLYC-AM and WILQ-FM, taking ownership of the stations on Aug. 1, 1975.

On the day of closing, with five months left in 1975, the stations were on track to produce about $375,000.00 in annual revenue.

By August 15 we were rolling out ideas, and for the year ending December 31, 1975 the stations had produced $437,000.00 in annual revenue.

On January 1, 1976 our books showed first-quarter booked business that was *double* what we'd projected when we made our 1976 forecast a week or so prior to the closing.

The jet was fueled and fully armed and we were on our way.

Looking back it is easy to see how the many lessons on programming and promotion Kerby and I learned from working for Susquehanna Broadcasting, the sales and management experience we gained under Marvin Mirvis' tutelage at WYRE, and the legal and accounting instruction given to us by Marvin Schein had combined to provide a solid foundation for running the business of a radio station.

When you choose to really focus on a goal it's amazing how things seem to fall into place 'automatically'. True focus is simply paying attention, and when you're paying attention, you're learning. For the longest time our goal had been 'owning a radio station together someday'. We were truly focused on that goal – 'paying attention' if you will.

As such, on August 1, 1975, we were more ready for station ownership than we could ever have imagined.

But there was more to learn. So much more.

CHAPTER 7
HAPPY NEW YEAR

Broadcasting Magazine showed 1975 Williamsport radio revenue at $770,000.00 spread among eleven radio stations. Our combined market share of that revenue was 57%!

In addition, January 1, 1976 showed us with more January and February business on the books (our 'carry') than the stations had produced for the same months in 1975—the *entire months*. This growth was far better than we would ever have expected.

We had created this momentum by selling ideas, and our ideas were producing results for our advertisers. Our radio stations were moving people to take action.

Our clients told us so.

Feathers

We decided that WILQ needed a 'character'.

The KGB Chicken was a great success. So, because we were a Country Music station (and I could do a passable imitation of Foghorn Leghorn) we created the WILQ Rooster.

Paul's 'infamous' WILQ Rooster spot

(with apologies to Warner Bros. Animation)
http://rlpublishers.com/WWW_Chap07-1.mp3

The 'Rooster Suit' was made by the same folks who made costumes for Disney. From the top of his comb to the tip o' his toes he was six-feet tall. Expensive, and worth every dime.

The WILQ Rooster was an instant hit! Children were drawn to him like shards to a magnet, and where the kids went the parents were sure to follow. Fact is, folks of all ages *loooved* having their pictures taken with this whacky bird. (There were no 'selfies' in 1976!)

The Rooster was only permitted to 'talk' in on-air promo announcements.

> *B...ahh say, Boyh. Ya need to be comin' to Juh – ahh say Jack Lowry Dodge this Saturday. Joe Dalto will be theah with lotsa priz – ahh sayh prizes, Son. C'mon out. And hey! Bring Mama Hen.*

Note: The WILQ Rooster was an instant 'star'. This worked so well for us that a 'character' became a part of nearly every radio station we acquired.

We paid $25.00 to whomever was in the costume for an on-location broadcast (a 'remote') – and we did a lot of 'em. Lee Troisi was the first Rooster.

'Extras' such as the Rooster and our station personalities appearing together at remotes (while dressing and behaving like professionals - imagine that!) quickly set us apart from the competition. We turned on-location broadcasts (I hate the term 'remote') into 'events' and these events quickly turned into a substantial source of revenue.

These broadcasts became so popular with advertisers we were soon doing two at a time, one on the 'C' (WLYC) and one on the 'Q' (WILQ). Our personalities were paid a $50.00 talent fee for hosting each two-hour broadcast.

1977 to 1979 my son Paul often drove the WILQ van to remotes carrying my youngest son, Peter, who 'starred' as 'The Rooster'. The boys also served as 'R&R Janitorial Service', cleaning/vacuuming the offices and emptying the wastebaskets each week. I got 'em in the business early.

At this writing both are still in radio. Paul is the Market President for the Clear Channel stations in Roanoke/Lynchburg, VA, and Peter is the Director of Sales for the Entercom stations in Gainesville, FL.

Indicators

There's always a measure of fear and trepidation when embarking on a new project. What you'd like to have is some tangible indication that you're actually on the right track, hopefully earlier rather than later.

We received two big ones. Really big!

Giant.

#1 - Big Numbers

One Late September day we received a call from an advertising agency. The caller said, “So…what is this WILQ radio station”?

“Huh? Whaaa…why do you ask”?

“Because WILQ showed up in the latest Arbitron ratings for Wilkes-Barre/Scranton and with really good numbers.”

“Not possible. WILQ has no signal in either of those cities. It must be a mistake.”

“No mistake. WILQ has great numbers, not in the Metro ratings but in the TSA (total service area).”

The Scranton/Wilkes-Barre TSA included Columbia, Montour and Northumberland counties, all of which were at the far end of WILQ’s ‘listenable’ signal. WILQ was the only FM station in a Country Music format.

Kerb and I got busy comparing the size of the population of these two counties with the number of Arbitron diaries that had been placed there.

Our math told us that the ‘Q’ *had* to have been listed in a majority of these diaries in order to achieve the sizable audience indicated by the ratings.

> *And if that’s the case - if the Q is that popular in these three ‘distant’ counties, how large might our audience be in the close-in counties – Lycoming, Sullivan and Union?*

As Kerby is fond of saying, "We were so excited our socks were rolling up and down our legs"!

We contacted Arbitron and negotiated a contract for them to conduct a Spring 1976 survey to include the counties of Lycoming, Union, Northumberland, Montour and Columbia counties.

#2 - Cookies and Cake-ies Alive Alive-O

Even better than the ratings good news was the response of our listeners.

On a near-daily basis 'the folks' would appear at the front desk bringing bags of cookies, or a cake, or a homemade fruit pie, or fudge, or sandwiches.

"Please give this to (fill in DJ's name here). We love his show and we love (fill in WILQ or WLYC here)."

No lie. We could have opened a bakery shop on the second floor of the Carone Building.

I'd never seen anything quite like this. We didn't just have *listeners.* Our stations had been 'adopted' by literally hundreds and hundreds of folks who showed us their love by bringing us goodies. Lots and lots of goodies!

Naturally our DJ's always thanked the folks by name, which served to add to the number of people bringing food and the variety of food being delivered.

Note: If you know anything at all about radio people you know that they are Foodies! Ya gotta believe our staff was in Hogg Heaven. Management too! Ya think they did that on purpose?

You should have seen what this looked like at holiday times, especially Valentine's Day, Thanksgiving and Christmas. It was astonishing!

I couldn't imagine anything better to prove that we were on the right track. To me our over-the-top effort to be 'in the community' rather than *locked inside the building* was the primary reason for this amazing listener reaction. This is at the top of my list titled 'How to build a great radio station'.

Note: Forty-five years later I'm still in touch with the folks at WILQ, including Program Director and Morning Host Ted Minier. I always ask Ted, "So…still gettin' cakes and cookies"? Last time I asked they were still on the right track!

Personal Growth

It was about this time I realized that our listeners were behaving more like our family. Our stations had been 'adopted' and made a part of their daily lives.

And I began to understand the uniqueness of radio broadcasting as a business, and the responsibility that fell to us as a result.

I came to believe that radio was one of the two or three most important members of any business community, especially in small and medium-sized markets.

Radio stations were privileged to present music, weather, news and entertainment. And of course some short 'newscasts' about various businesses. (You know…'Commercials'?)

But far more important was (and still is) the obligation to be 'at the ready' when things get out of order: major weather problems, floods, fires and all kinds of other important local and regional situations. And to be there when things were going swimmingly, providing on-air promotion of and actual physical involvement with local expos, school and church events, fireworks displays, club events (Rotary, Kiwanis, Lions) and so forth.

As I progressed thru this epiphany (and because radio can talk) I began to view radio stations as living breathing beings, the various 'organs' of which are members of the stations' staff. (Radio stations were never meant to be 'music machines'.)

As for our listeners and our communities, well, 'they only need us when they need us'. As such, we'd better be always alive. Always aware. Always 'ready'.

This philosophy became the foundation of my thinking and the root of everything Kerby and I did for the next many years. I believe it to this day.

Note: I adore small and medium-market radio. If you're doing what you're supposed to be doing, i.e. making a difference, your listeners will become your family and your business will flourish. You will do well by doing good.

OK – I'm down off my soapbox.

Simple Yet Elegant

Most of the businesses in the Susquehanna Valley were 'grounded' in the use of newspaper, many to the exclusion of radio. Placement of their newspaper ads was as routine as brushing their teeth (which I assumed many of them were doing). It was automatic. They did it 'by rote'.

To this add the fact that each town had one newspaper but several radio stations (owned by several different companies) and you can see why placing a newspaper ad was easy.

Compare one meeting with a newspaper rep with listening to pitches from three, four or five different media sales reps who were busy trashing their competitors - and thus radio in general - instead of concentrating on how their station can improve the prospect's business. And by the way – trashing competitors was a no-no in our company. When during a client or listener meeting the subject of a competitor came up our staff was instructed to say, "We think WXXY is a fine station. Now please let me tell you what we have for you today." Or something similar.

Ya Wanna Bet?

Many times our prospective customers would give us myriad reasons why they didn't want to use our product, the most frequent of which was, "Radio doesn't work."

We set out to prove 'em wrong.

I hung a month-by-month Happy Day Calendar in the sales office and instructed our sales people to put the name of any prospect who'd said anything that sounded like "Radio doesn't work" under any Monday thru Friday day on the calendar.

Only one 'in denial' prospect per weekday. First come first served.

Each day we put a 3 x 5 card on the in-studio console bulletin board with instructions to read the card exactly as written. No added comments. No additions. No subtractions. Exactly as written.

> "Today is Bill Castle Day on WILQ (or WLYC). If you see Bill, tell him to have a Happy Day."

Just that. I gave our DJ's specific instructions to "Say it *exactly* that way."

Never 'Tell him to have a Happy Day *from WILQ*.' NO!

Why?

Because after he gets a lot of calls we want ol' Bill to have to investigate. You know...ask a bunch of questions to find out where in the world this is coming from. Hopefully Bill will ask his friend about this and the friend will say, “I heard it on WILQ (or WLYC).”

> "Wait Paul. Are you sure Bill will get calls and/or in-person mentions"?

There’s nary a doubt in my mind.

To be certain that this was done every hour without fail we had traffic add a Happy Day entry on each hour of the program log – 6AM to 8 PM, Monday thru Friday.

> “Sooo, how did this work, Aggravation Breath?”

Almost immediately we began to get calls from our unsuspecting Happy Dayers asking us whathehell was going on?

> “I got ten or fifteen calls this morning about some Happy Day somethin’rother. What’s that all about”?

Before this turned into complaints I cut the mentions back to every other hour.
I had to. The response was driving the honorees crazy!

Point made! This was just one way we turned a bunch of business people into radio believers.

1976

Based on the way we’d ended business in 1975 we decided to shoot for $550,000.00 in 1976, a 26% increase.

All we had upon which to base this projection was the way the stations had performed in the final five months of 1975. It surely wasn’t based on our ‘vast experience’ as owner-operators.

And it could never have been based on the fact that Williamsport and the Susquehanna Valley was a 'growth market' - because it wasn't.

But hey. Nothing ventured, nothing gained!

The Image Makers

Troisi's Men's Shop had been a downtown Williamsport fixture for years and was now owned by Bob and John Troisi, two of the founder's sons. The shop was small in size but large in stylish inventory.

I loved the store and told Bob and John I thought they should be using our radio stations. They said their advertising 'plan' rested on using the back page of the *Williamsport Sun-Gazette Newspaper,* which they'd been doing for years.

"OK John," sez I, "But ya know what? I bet after all these years everyone who's seen your ad and decided to visit your store has probably already done so. Wouldn't you agree"?

John said, "Hmm. I never looked at it that way before."

"I think you need to start talking to a different group of men and I have an idea that will fit you perfectly. Can we get together next Wednesday? Won't take more than twenty minutes. How about eight-thirty...so I'm not interrupting you after the store opens."

"See you Wednesday."

Back at the station I went through the TM jingles and found one that was specifically created for a men's store.

Sixty-second version:

> *TM jingle singers*: "The Image Makers Where the Look is Yours."

Short musical bed, then: "The Image Makers."

35 second musical bed, then: "The Image Makers where the look is yours."
Short musical bed, then: "The Image Makers."

I produced a presentation similar to the one I'd done for English's in 1974, dubbed it to a cassette and played it for Bob and John.

They flipped out.

Short version: I convinced John to simply drop 30% of their back-page ads and use the money for spots on our stations – no increase in their ad budget.

We had the jingle customized to sing their names.

TM Jingle Singers: "The Image Makers Where the Look is Yours. Bob and John Troisi. The Image Makers."

By 1977 they'd cut their newspaper usage by 75% and were using over one thousand spots annually on our two stations.

Did It Work?

In 1979 John told me that use of radio and their jingle had resulted in a doubling of their gross revenue in just three years.

Proof Of The Pudding

In 1979 the postman delivered a letter to John at the store. The envelope was addressed thusly:

The Image Makers
Williamsport, PA

One That Went Away...Literally

Even though we'd only been at it for ten months or so, Kerby was always on the lookout for opportunities. He'd stayed in touch with Joe Sitrick and Jim Blackburn, each of whom was an agent with Blackburn and Company, a leading brokerage firm handling radio and television station sales. Apparently my ever-effusive partner had told them about how well we were doing and that we might be looking to make another acquisition.

In mid-June of 1976 we got a call from Jim Blackburn. He told us of an AM/FM combo for sale in Lynchburg, VA, allowing that "...this one is right up your alley and it's priced to sell." I must say, I had no thoughts that we were ready to expand quite yet but whattheheck - let's take a look.

We made an appointment for a Monday in early July. The following Sunday Kerby and I and our wives headed for a hotel in Lynchburg.

Oh Oh

Next morning Kerb and I grabbed some breakfast and waited for Jim Blackburn in the hotel lobby. He arrived around 8:30 with a puzzled look on his face.

"Hey guys, I have some sorta bad news. The owner's gonna be late for our meeting today. He spent the weekend in jail."

Muhhwhaaat? Jail?

"Yeah. He's having some personal problems. Nothing violent but his wife had him thrown in the clink. He'll be here around ten."

Sooo...we're standing in front of the hotel around ten when up pulls a powder-blue Mercedes Benz two-seater with a navy blue top. Sweet!

And out steps a fellow wearing a beautifully tailored, very expensive suit...complete with wrinkled dress shirt and a three-day growth of beard.

Brief introductions, then it's off to see the stations.

Fifteen minutes later we arrived at a neat-looking studio/office building located at the transmitter site – towers standing tall behind the building. We had a quick walk thru the office space ('ya seen one ya seen 'em all') after which we followed the owner to his office.

The door to his office was located 'lower left' of the room. The back wall of the office was all windows overlooking the Blue Ridge Mountains of Virginia - a beautiful view.

The owner's large desk was to the right of the door about ten feet in front of the back wall. His chair was behind the desk, facing the windows.

After entering the office, in order to get to his desk, he had to walk straight into the room toward the windows, turn right at the front of the desk, turn right again at the end of the desk, walk a few steps toward the back wall then turn right and sit in the chair.

This route to the desk was a guided pathway, 'walled' on both sides by stacks of books, file folders, random piles of loose papers and some boxes, probably containing more of the same.

Scattered on top of his desk were newspapers, accounting books, some random one-page charts, file folders and scattered assorted unidentifiable papers...

...and checks. Lots of checks. Uncashed. Presumably client payment for advertising schedules.

Prominently displayed at the front of the desk was a rather large triangular shaped wooden piece, one that in most cases would feature a person's name in gold lettering.

Not this time.

Instead, printed in gold lettering in Italian-American-accented lingo was:

Doan'ah Clean Uppa Mah Desk, You Mess Uppa My System!

Have A Seat

Somewhere in the mess were three chairs, all covered with more papers.

"Have a seat," he said. "Just put that stuff on the floor. Don't worry about it."

And right there…right in the midst of the chaos…we negotiated a purchase price. Kerby and I agreed to get a contract to him within a week. We shook hands, said our goodbyes and departed.

Back To Billtown

Our lawyer drew up the contract and sent it to Jim Blackburn for distribution.

Sidebar: I wasn't exactly sure how we proposed to pay for this acquisition. Kerb was confident.

'Tweren't Meant To Be

We expected to hear something from the owner soon after he received the contract. After all, no one ever signs the 'first draft' of a contract, right?

Crickets!

On the following Monday I called Jim Blackburn to check the progress.

"Oh, hey Paul, I was just getting ready to call you. The deal's off. The owner took his own life on Friday."

[Holy ...!]

'Tis all true I swear.

Just another wild-assed radio deal gone awry.

Providence

At this point we were not yet familiar with the vital importance of antenna height and terrain, with regard to its effect on an FM radio station signal. The mountainous terrain in and around Lynchburg was/is an unfixable problem for FM radio stations. Not knowing this would have proven to be a disaster for us at this stage of our ownership careers.

Not getting these stations was a blessing.

Fairly soon, we were to receive this lesson in spades.

Can't Quit Now.

Undaunted, we stayed in acquisition mode by attempting to buy a stand-alone AM station in Reading, PA. *[Details in the next chapter.]*

Great Days Ahead

Late July/early August brought us incredible 'career-changing' news.

The result of the Spring, 1976 Arbitron ratings for the Williamsport/Lycoming County Metro showed WILQ with a 28 share and WLYC had a twelve, a combined forty-share of radio listeners, mostly adults 25-54—the 'money demographic'.

Note: WILQ's ratings in the multiple county Total Survey Area (TSA) were even more impressive.

We owned a pair of ratings juggernauts.

Note: A year or two later I was told that WILQ was the highest Arbitron-rated Country station east of the Mississippi – ...raht theah in good ol' Weeahmspoaht, By Gawd, Pennsilvane-Eye-A!

CHAPTER 8
DREAMLAND

Our stations continued to grow at a record pace and the next three years absolutely flew by – a fast-paced dream. Like, Indy-500 speed dream.

I'd do it all over again in a skinny minute!

Schooling

It wasn't long before Kerby and I realized that the 'education' we'd received while working for Susquehanna Broadcasting and its President, Arthur W. Carlson, was probably the very best thing that could ever have happened for us.

First on the list was their 'strip-marketing' concept: The market is *not* the city of license or even the county wherein the station resides. Rather, it's every Burg, Town, City or County that is covered by the listenable signal of the radio station.

At WSBA, the York, Lancaster and Harrisburg areas (the 'strip market') were always referred to on-air as 'WSBA Land'. At WARM we called all of North-Eastern Pennsylvania 'WARM Land'. For WILQ Kerby and I chose 'The Susquehanna Valley,' the vast area that WILQ covered like a blanket.

We instructed our on-air staff to mention our city of license, Williamsport, only in FCC-mandated top-of-the-hour station breaks and at other times when the city required mentioning, as in a news story, a commercial or the location of an out-of-station event.

Speaking of which...second on the list of 'Lessons Learned from Susquehanna Broadcasting' was 'get the radio stations out of the studio and into the communities'. Susquehanna wrote the book on this important factor.

As On-Air Talent, Kerby and I participated in a lot of this action and paid very close attention to all that it contributed to the success of the giant radio stations where we were employed.

I can't say what the other DJs were seeing and thinking, but because of our long-term goal I believe Kerby and I were unconsciously measuring things as we looked forward to the day when we'd also be owner-operators.

We could not have asked for better instructors.

Hot Stuff

January thru March is the slowest time of the year for radio ad sales - lots of inventory available but a dearth of buyers. Susquehanna (there we go again!) had devised a sales-oriented promotion to increase their first-quarter business. They called it the Zodiac. We 'researched' the idea.

I changed the name Zodiac to "GRABBER: The Great Radio Advertisers Booze Banquet and Entertainment Rally" and we were off and running.

We created affordable first-quarter ad packages to offer local businesses (three months worth for $465 to $625 per package), made arrangements to trade several big prizes, and started selling.

The advertiser was charged with just two requirements: One, all GRABBER Package spots had to be aired by March 31st and paid for by May 1. Two, In order to win prizes the owner or the 'main principal' of the business had to be in attendance at the banquet.

We had no idea how (or if) this would be accepted.

Fire! Aim! Ready!

Wow! Our stellar sales staff moved these first-quarter packages at an alarming rate. Surprisingly, many advertisers wanted to purchase multiple packages—a testament to the success they were realizing from advertising with us.

We decided to limit sales to one hundred packages, no more than three packages per client.

(Too late! On the day we made this decision our sellers brought in contracts for packages #105 and #106!)

The Nitty Gritty

For each package purchased the advertiser got one 'prize ticket' (there were one-hundred six of those) and two seats at the banquet tables.

For the banquet we worked a trade deal with a local hotel.

For prizes, we traded or purchased a selection of ninety-one nice items valued at $10 to $20 dollars ($60.00 to $70.00 in today's money).

We traded the remaining fifteen prizes, working upward from a prize valued at $40.00 to the 'biggie' valued at three to four-thousand dollars (*to establish 2019 valuation multiply X 4*).

Note: By 'trade' I mean trading radio advertising for goods or services of equal value. We concentrated on trading with businesses that would only use our stations in that manner, seldom if ever trading with cash-paying advertisers.

The GRABBER Banquet

Cocktails were served starting at 6 PM. Attendees were seated at seven.

A table sat on the stage in the front of the room. Behind the table stood a very large corked billboard.

On the table was a large clear-glass bowl containing one-hundred and six cards, each with the name of a GRABBER sponsor - one card for each package purchased. Tacked on the billboard was an equal number of consecutively arranged cards, with the name of a prize printed on each.

Prizes numbered sixteen to one hundred six were the $10 to $20-dollar prizes. Those numbered from fifteen to one were of considerably higher value. #1 was the biggie.

The Drawing

We started the drawing during dessert. Our DJs handled it with flair.

Example: Joe Dalto took card #106 off the billboard and Lori Shannon took a card from the bowl.

Jim Cameron: "All right! Here is a match made in heaven! Prize #106, a $15.00 gift certificate from Johnny's Tastee Freeze goes to...Ta Daa!...Ticket #37, Montour Auto Supply." (*cheers/groans).*

Staff members took turns with the drawings and announcements.

"Prize #105. A $20.00 gift certificate from Helmrich's Seafood Market goes to...Drum Roll Please! Jack Lowry Dodge." *(more cheers/groans).*

In an effort to keep interest up we awarded prizes at a rate of seven to ten every two minutes. About every seventh or eighth drawing was for one of the prizes numbered from #15 to # 6 – nice gifts but not the five biggies.

We saved them for last!

Cheers and groans got louder and louder as we awarded the prizes...folks realizing that they were either still in it for the Biggies...or had lost all hope.

At 'Final Five' time there were five cards on the board and five cards in the bowl. Everyone in the room knew who was 'still alive'.

We awarded prize #5 (*Yaaay!/Booo!),* then #4, then #3, leaving only #2 and #1. As I recall: Prize #2 was in the $1,500.00 range, and first prize was a nice boat and trailer; the winner of Prize #2 was a client who'd bought multiple packages; Prize #1 was taken down by a small advertiser who'd purchased just one.

The place went nuts!

A Smash Hit

Our outstanding staff was dressed to the nines. They looked great and handled the drawing like they'd done it a hundred times.

We went First Class with the Open Bar Cocktail Hour and the fine dinner and dessert. The prizes were top drawer. This got rave reviews.

Clients and staff enjoyed one another's company in a non-business setting. Invaluable!

We generated over $45,000.00 in first-quarter revenue with out of pocket costs of less than $4,000.00. I believe our stations were two of a small handful of radio stations that were profitable in that particular first quarter.

The best news? Our clients let us know that they expected to be back next year.

Many were.

Confession: Two years later I 'caved' to a growing sense of propriety and changed the name to 'The Great Radio Advertisers Bountiful Banquet and Entertainment Rally'. I know, I know. I oughtta be ashamed of myself.

$tation Promotion$

Kerby and I always believed we should make our station promotions 'revenue positive' whenever possible. We achieved this goal by partnering with clients.

Example: If other radio stations had a nice boat or a dynamite vacation to give away they most likely would have some kind of 'be the fifth caller and get qualified to win' scheme, after which they'd draw someone's name out of a hat and give 'em the prize. I think stations believed this somehow made the contest more 'pure' and therefore more desirable. I *know* that many of the DJs saw it that way.

Puh-leeze! You really think *listeners* knew the difference – or would have cared either way?

That's just nuts.

Not us.

Example: If we had a boat and trailer to give away we'd put a "Win The Boat" package together and take it to various clients, designating them as locations where folks could go to register to win the boat.

Oftentimes the package would include one or two 'on-location' broadcasts (a 'Boat Remote'?) featuring one of our personalities and the WILQ Rooster. The boat would be on display and folks could register to win.

The boat would be first prize but we'd also have lesser nice prizes to give away, one prize for each participating client.

At the end of the contest we'd collect the registration boxes from each client and draw one slip from each box. That winner got one of the nice 'lesser prizes.'

Then we dumped all entries into a big container, mixed 'em up and drew one slip. That person would win the boat.

So…a boat that we (probably) traded for otherwise-unsold advertising we turned into thousands of dollars in revenue.

Again, listeners wouldn't know (or care) whether we turned a profit. What they *knew* was that this stuff was fun…and folks won prizes.

'Nuff said.

Bumper Stickers

In 1976 we decided on a bumper-sticker campaign for our spring/summer promotion. We put together a *(you guessed it)* Bumper Sticker package, this one co-sponsored by two clients.

On the air we promoted participating clients' locations where folks could get the stickers, then devised several ways to give away stuff.

Our listeners never seemed to tire of our bumper sticker promotions. We loved 'em too.

A year or two later we included couponing. Printed on the removable backing of our stickers were two money-saving coupons, one for each of our two major sponsors – paid for of course.

We did this several times from 1976 to 1981. One year it was the WILQ Rooster Booster Bumper Sticker.

Observational Insight

At around five-fifteen on a rainy late-November afternoon in 1979 our Sales Manager, Mike Steinhilper, and I were standing by the large second floor windows in our offices, overlooking the traffic passing by on West Fourth Street in Williamsport.

Many of the cars, SUVs and Ford F-150s had one or more of our WILQ stickers affixed to their bumpers. Plenty of these vehicles had young passengers or were being driven by younger people.

After watching this scene for a minute or two I said to Mike, "By 1985 or '86 Country Music will be the fastest-growing music format in America and will probably be Number One by the late eighties."

Mike said, "Why do you say that?"

"Look at the number of cars and trucks that have WILQ bumper stickers and then look at the age of the people driving or riding in these vehicles. Ya gotta believe they're listening to the 'Q', right? Fifteen years ago in this part of the country you couldn't get anyone under the age of fifty to admit that they liked country music. Today the younger people are getting exposed to it earlier than ever before. Look at our ratings. If Country is this big in North Central Pennsylvania how big do you think it is in the south and the mid-west? I'm telling you – Number One in the next five to seven years."

Kerby and I backed that belief many times, always successfully. Evidence to follow.

A Lesson In The Law

Every now and then we found ourselves in a minor pee-pee contest with George Vajda. Never anything serious, always avoidable – but usually just enough to create a good case of acid stomach.

One spring morning - a day when my friend and company attorney, Marvin Schein, Esq. was in town - the mailman delivered a George 'panties in a wad' letter.

"You are late with your note payment. I'm going to sue you."

The letter was signed, "Cordially, George."

[*Insert laugh here.*]

Our always on-time payment and George's letter probably crossed in the mail, but just the presumptuousness of his note had knocked me a bit off kilter.

So…Marvin and I are walking up West Fourth Street and I'm going on about how stupid this letter is. "I think I'll sue him for harassment," sez I. "This crap is unnecessary. I'll take him to court and beat his butt."

Marvin looked at me and said, "Oh yeah? Well there's something you need to understand. Nothing is cut and dried in the law."

The incident was unremarkable. Marvin's ultra-succinct observation was spot on.

WILQ/WLYC Wrap Up

We continued to set sales and ratings records and marveled as WILQ became a regional broadcast giant. Here's a couple examples of how.

Pet Rocks. In 1977, on a late-in-the-season Christmas challenge, we helped Neyhart's sell four or five dozen Pet Rocks in less than a week.

I wrote a thirty-second spot – a Q&A that would serve to turn a formerly 'never radio' business into a regular client.

Q: "What adorable little pet always sits quietly and looks at you with loving eyes"?

A: "A pet rock."

Q: "What pet never needs a bath or a grooming"?

A: "A pet rock."

Q: "What is the best stocking gift you'll ever see"?

A: "A pet rock."

(More Q&A to the conclusion.)

Q: "So where can I get a pet rock"?

A: "Only at Neyharts on Third Street in Williamsport. But you'd better hurry. They're going fast."

Or something like that.

Penn State Football. I became friendly with Fran Fisher, at that time the voice of Penn State football. A local AM station had the broadcast rights to the games and I wanted 'em. I convinced

Fran that he needed to have the broadcasts on a big-footprint FM station rather than exclusively on a small footprint Class 4 AM. I told Fran I didn't mind if the other station continued broadcasting the games.

We landed the FM rights to the broadcasts which enabled us to sell otherwise 'near-give-away' Saturday inventory for top rates. This was great programming for us and it gave our Sports Director, the late Bill Keen, an opportunity to display his considerable talent.

Hands-on Contest. In the center court of the Lycoming Mall we presented 'Put Your Hands On The Car', a smash-hit promotion that would not be allowed in today's environment.

We traded for a new car with a local dealer, then we sold 'Put Your Hands' packages to local businesses where folks registered to participate in the contest. One person was chosen from each participating client, plus five contestants who won via on-air.

The contest started on a Friday evening. At 7 PM each contestant placed a hand on the car. Other than two thirty-minute breaks each day, any time a contestant broke contact with the car they eliminated themselves.

The last person with a hand on the car would win the car. Second prize was an all-expense paid 'long weekend' in New Orleans.

This went on for almost three full days. By late Monday afternoon there were two people with 'hands on' - a man and a woman.

Finally, at the point of his maximum exasperation the man was heard to exclaim rather loudly, "Screw this. I'm going to New Orleans."

He took his hand off the car and the lady was the winner!

By 1977, WILQ was established as the run-away number one radio station in the five counties that we called 'The Susquehanna Valley'.

Uh Oh

In 1978 a competitor with a full-time AM signal changed to a pure Top Forty format, sealing the doom of our daytime-only WLYC.

Wasting no time fighting a battle that I knew we'd never win, we immediately changed WLYC's format to Al Hamm's 'Music Of Your Life'.

This format was aimed at the largest age demographic in Lycoming County - Adults 50+. WLYC revenue immediately dropped by thirty percent, then totally stabilized. It became an 'easy sell' to many business owners because they liked the music.

(Yet another huge lesson: In small markets your clients are also your listeners, many of whom will tend to spend ad dollars with stations they like with no regard for the ratings. That turned out to be the case with The New WLYC.)

Meanwhile, WILQ revenue continued to soar.

In 1979, I was honored to be elected Volunteer President of the Williamsport-Lycoming Chamber of Commerce. I also MC'd our annual dinner at which Charles Osgood was the featured speaker, a mega-talent who loved radio. He was terrific.

Revenue Explosion

In 1979, WILQ and WLYC produced gross revenue of $1,287,500.00, as gross radio revenue for Williamsport overall approached two-million dollars. Kerby and I and our fine staff had made quite a difference indeed.

And we were back on the acquisition trail.

WHUM (you'll love this)

Circa 1976: Reading, PA was the epitome of an 'under-radioed' market - just five viable local stations for Berks County, three of which were AMs. (*AM was still a force and would remain so until the mid-1980s.*) We saw this as a great opportunity to roll out a Country format where none existed, hoping to duplicate our success with WILQ.

Our FCC counsel, Jason L. Shrinsky Esq., represented us in the deal that proved to be a real adventure.

I can't recall the exact purchase price for the station, but I do remember that the seller wanted $100,000.00 paid to him in cash at closing—an amount to be 'unmentioned' in the purchase agreement, and as sworn to in the documents that would be filed with the FCC.

Example: Say the actual purchase price was $600,000.00. The document would certify that the price was $500,000.00, but there would be a 'wink, wink $100K' paid to the seller in cash at closing.

You know. Like...under the table?

(It was apparent to me that the guy had partners with whom he didn't want to 'share the swag'. What other reason could there have been?)

Our FCC Counsel was Jason L. Shrinsky, ESQ who prepared the contract and all of the required FCC filings.

Kerby and I didn't know how to handle the sellers' *request* (demand?) for this payment to which we'd already agreed. We explained this to Jason who said, "Don't give this another minutes thought. Relax. I'll handle it."

The Post-Closing Adventure

Following a several-month wait we received FCC approval to complete the transfer of control and a closing date was set. The closing went off without a hitch.

Comes Now The 'Wink, Wink'

After the closing Jason, Kerby and I stood in the hallway waiting for the elevator. The seller sidled up beside us as the elevator arrived and we all got on board.

As the door was closing the seller gave us an "Ahem" and 'mentioned' his cash payment.

With a horrified look on his face Shrinsky said (incredulously), "Why...we could *never* do anything like that. You know that the FCC filing has all of us certifying that $500,000.00 was the total purchase price for the station and that there was no other consideration whatsoever. You signed these documents. We all did.

"If the FCC learned that we gave anyone additional consideration they'd find us guilty of fraud and void the transaction. Surely you don't want that to happen, right"?

(I told you he was a great lawyer.)

The silence was deafening.

We never heard from the seller again.

Meet The Management

Kerby and I were now out of the elevator and on to the station's studios and offices, located in the ultimate low-rent district – the basement of an old hotel in downtown Reading, adjoining the boiler room.

I can't recall the name of the hotel - The Berkshire Towers maybe.

(Nice location. Listeners will love to visit. NOT!)

Prior to the closing we'd met most of the management and staff. When we arrived (around 11:45 am) we asked to see the Station Manager.

"He's out at the moment."

"When is he expected back?"

"Probably tomorrow morning. He gets here around eight but he leaves around 11:30 to go to his real estate office."

(Whaaat? You're kidding.)

"Ahmmm…OK. How about the Sales Manager."

"Oh, he's gone for lunch. He'll be back around 2:15."

"Gee…three hours? Seems like a bit long for a lunch."

"Well, after lunch he watches his favorite soap opera. It's on from one 'til two."
(No wonder the station was for sale!)

Kerby and I were floored. We excused ourselves and repaired to a nearby restaurant for lunch and conversation.

It took us about fifteen minutes to decide that we needed to find a manager and a sales manager.

Quickly!

Henry And David – East

Oh wait. Those other guys are *Harry* and David. Right.

Anyway…we hired Henry E. Kirk IV and David Bernstein to be our management team – Henry as General Manager and Dave as Sales Manager.

Short Ending

This was decidedly *not* a pairing that would result in these two gentlemen being seen someday selecting furniture together, but they did a fabulous job in turning WHUM profitable.

Quick Sidebar: In 1979 Dave hired an outstanding young man named Scott Swift *for our sales staff. In no time at all Scott became the sales leader for WHUM, and showed excellent potential for future management and partnership opportunities with us.*

In 1981, Kerby and I purchased an FM station in Greenville, SC (more to come) and asked Dave to be our partner and General Manager.

With that in mind I headed to Reading to offer the job of WSSL (né WGXL) Sales Manager to Scott.

Before I could get the words out of my mouth he said, "Paul, I'm handing in my resignation today. I've taken a job with Merrill-Lynch."

Our loss was Merrill's gain.

Scott Swift was a real talent who went on to have a fabulous career with that company and also to father a very talented young woman.

Ms Taylor Swift.

Another Quick Sidebar: By 1981 FM was rapidly overtaking AM. Kerby and I realized we had a short window to 'get outta Dodge' with our pocketbooks intact.

In late 1981 we took a small profit and sold WHUM.

This was the last stand-alone AM we would buy.

Note: In retrospect, WILQ and WLYC turned out to be our 'laboratory'. We were fortunate to be able to 'learn on the job' while building a very successful business. No lessons learned in business are more powerful than those learned via trial and error and 'hands on'. The time we spent in this 'lab' and the lessons we learned there were of immeasurable help to us as we built our company that would soon be known as Keymarket Communications.

CHAPTER 9
ON TO THE NEXT

In February of 1977 Dick Kozacko called with an opportunity. WKRT AM/FM licensed to Cortland, NY was being offered for sale.

The stations were owned and operated by Mr. Leighton Hope, a fine gentleman who also owned Greek Peak, a ski area in Cortland. Both radio stations were excellent facilities.

WKRT-AM broadcast @ 920 kc with 1 kw daytime and .5 kw at night.

The FM was a full Class B, licensed to broadcast with 50 kw @ an antenna height of 500 feet HAAT (Height Above Average Terrain).

Dick was excited about this because he knew the FM tower was short and could be heightened, after which the 65 dbu signal would cover not only Cortland County but also Tompkins County and Ithaca, NY — about eighteen miles to the east and the home of both Cornell University and Ithaca College. (Cortland was home to a college as well - SUNY-Cortland.)

I can't remember the asking price but I do recall that Kerby and I thought this might be an opportunity, an affordable one at that.

We made an appointment to visit.

Monopoly

These were the only radio stations licensed to Cortland County, meaning that without competition there was little incentive to go overboard with activity and/or creativity — a way in which we did not know how to behave.

Interestingly, the stations sounded OK and the station staff seemed to be alert and interested in what they were doing.

The further good news? The stations were simulcast. To us this meant that one of the two excellent radio signals was being totally wasted.

We made an offer. It was accepted.

Elvis...And A Long Day In Syracuse

After hammering out a Letter of Intent we made arrangements with Jason Shrinsky to represent us in finalizing the contract, which was scheduled to take place at the Syracuse offices of Mr. Hope's legal representatives. Around ten AM I met Jason at the Syracuse airport and off we went.

With only the skeleton of an agreement in place, we were faced with creating an entire Asset Purchase Agreement from scratch. Granted, much of it was boilerplate, but details are never easy...and we had a lot of details to go thru.

Short version: We started at 11 AM and finally had a signed contract around 10:15 PM. (*Whew!*)

To Go, Or Not To Go...

That was the question.

Jason had a late plane to Washington, DC and I had a decision to make. After dropping Jason at the airport I sat in my car for a few minutes.

(Do I head for home or do I get a hotel room and leave in the morning?)

Finding a hotel would take about ten minutes, whilst a drive home would be a bit shy of four hours. If I left now I'd be home around three AM.

I decided to go for it.

By the time I found my way out of Syracuse it was close to midnight. I stopped at a late night diner, grabbed a cup of coffee and headed for Williamsport.

Late Night DX-ing

Naturally, I turned on my radio. Every station was playing Elvis records, one right after the other…and no one was talking.

"Something's happened to Elvis," sez I, as my Pink Panther side emerged.

Around 1:30 I landed on WWWE (called 'Three Double-U E'), a 50 kw clear channel AM out of Cleveland, Ohio.

The night jock came out of 'I Can't Stop Falling In Love With You'. "The king is dead. Elvis Presley, dead of a drug overdose at age 42."

Wow!

Elvis' death made it easy for me to remember this day, the way those things get frozen in time in your mind.

Note: I saw Elvis perform 'on stage' at the Baltimore Civic Center in (probably) 1974, backed up by Sissy Houston and The Sweet Inspirations. I'll never forget how the darkened building suddenly became bright as day when Elvis emerged from stage left and thousands of flash-bulbs went off simultaneously. Impressive!

Management

We closed on the stations early in 1978. We recruited our friend Don Kelley to be our partner and General Manager, and promoted Bob Jackson (from our Williamsport stations) to be the Sales Manager. The Kelly/Jackson 'forced management team' simply did not work. Think oil mixed with water. Not very long into our ownership Don hired Bill McMartin to replace Bob Jackson as Sales Manager.

These two made a great team. In fact, McMartin was so good that it wasn't long before he was offered a similar job at a big station in Syracuse, which he accepted. As he should have.

Note: In later years Don owned radio stations in PA and NJ. Last time I checked Bill was an executive with Clear Channel.

WNOZ

We figured the 'bonus market' in this deal was the large cadre of college students attending the aforementioned three schools, so we decided to make WKRT-FM a 'rock' station.

We changed the call letters to WNOZ - called 'The Nose'. The logo below sez it all!

This led to the use of many 'outrageous' (for the times) breakers and liners, the most obnoxious of which was: "Hey!

When someone asks you about your favorite radio station…just smile and say, 'I pick the Nose'."

Oh well. You had to be there!

The Grant…And The Groan

We decided to build a taller tower on the land where our present tower was standing. Our consulting engineer assured us that our signal would easily cover Ithaca.

The new license was granted without a hitch. The new tower build took about three months. At last, it was time to hang the antenna and blast that flame-throwing signal over Ithaca!

'Hang The Antenna Day' found me in my office in Williamsport, anxiously anticipating the call from Don Kelley…the one that told me The Nose was 'blowing' a signal all over Ithaca. (Sorry. I couldn't resist!)

Around 9:30 my phone rang.

"Don Kelly is on line one."

"Hey Don!"

"You can't hear it," Don whispered.

"What did you say"?

'You can't hear it."

"You gotta be kidding. You can't hear it"?

"Paul, I'm in downtown Ithaca and there's no audible signal."

"I'll be there in two hours."

There's Something Called 'A Terrain Study'

I left the office, went home, threw some stuff in a suitcase and was off to Ithaca.

The last leg of the trip was a forty-mile drive up Rt. 13 from Horseheads, NY to Ithaca, the terrain slowly rising the entire time. About twenty miles west of Ithaca (and a full fifty miles from the antenna) 'The Nose' was booming in, loud and clear.

(What the 'H!')

OK…so the town of Ithaca is located at the foot of Cayuga Lake, one of the eleven deep cold water lakes – the Finger Lakes, that were gouged out of the landscape by the powerful forces unleashed during the Ice Age.

There exists a 200-foot drop from the elevated terrain on either side of Ithaca to the populated area 'down where the folks are'. I'd driven thru there many times before and never gave it a thought.

The closer I got to Ithaca the louder the station sounded. I was confused.

Eventually I arrived at the top of the hill just southwest of Ithaca and began my long descent into the city. About halfway down this deep descent into the city the station went silent.

Ulp! – *I couldn't hear it!*

I couldn't hear the station – at all.

And the worst part was I had no idea why.

The Lesson

A quick conversation with our engineer revealed the problem.

That Ice Age had created this huge deep gulch with no regard whatsoever as to how that would affect our someday FM signal!

How dare it.

To quote Louie DePalma in the TV show *'Taxi'* "What to do...what to do"?

We made a deal to hang an auxiliary antenna on the tower of a heating oil company – the tower being located at the edge of the hill looking straight down into Ithaca. Not the same as having our 'flame-throwing' main signal all over the market but better than nothing by a mile.

Problem solved, right?

Not quite!

Shortly after we hung the auxiliary antenna one of the jocks from an Ithaca competitor put us off the air by setting fire to the building owned by the oil company wherein resided not only our transmitter but those transmitters used by the oil company to communicate with their drivers.

It seems he was in a local tavern, drinking beer and bitching about the fact that 'this damned Cortland station is trying to steal our listeners and grab our revenue. Someone needs to burn down their transmitter building'.

Whoops!

FCC licenses are federally granted and regulated so tampering with a radio station is a felony.

The authorities nabbed 'our boy'.

I seem to recall he ended up using some of his vacation time as a guest of Uncle Sam - 'in stir.'

Several weeks later the transmitter was back on the air.

In the end this arrangement allowed the station to be competitive in Ithaca, but it never dominated as it might otherwise have done.

Note. Kerby and I concluded that our consulting engineer must have simply used a compass and a road map and, without giving a thought to the terrain, he put the point on the map where our antenna would be and drew a circle 45 miles in diameter, showing that the station would throw a good signal over Ithaca. Which it did. High over Ithaca!

This experience led us to always...*always* require terrain studies when planning to re-locate FM radio stations.

In the next seven years we went on to build more than ten tall-towers and never made another terrain mistake.

The 'Cortland Lesson' saved us many headaches and lots of money going forward.

Whaaat?

In late August of 1978 Kerby came into our office and said, "What would you do if I died"?

"Huh"? *(Where in the hell did that come from?)*

He repeated the question.

"I guess I'd keep on running radio stations like I've been doing. Why do you ask? Are you ill? What's up"?

"No...I'm not ill. But Jerry Atchley and Jim Long have found an FM for sale in Little Rock, Arkansas. They want me to partner with them and go down there and run the station."

Jim Long was President of TM Productions, an industry-leading Dallas-based company that produced jingles and ad/promotional campaigns for radio stations and businesses all over North America. Jerry Atchley was the TM Sales Manager. To say I was nonplussed would be a gross understatement.

My mind was racing. I had a lot of questions. The first of which was "Whatthehellisgoingonhere?"

I was absolutely stunned that Kerby would even consider doing a deal with another partner let alone starting to makes plans to do so.

My next thought was "Hell, we just acquired two markets. Don't you think we have enough to do?" followed by "So, you'd expect that we'd continue to co-own these stations but I'd be running them and you off somewhere else?"

And last: "I thought we had an agreement that it's just us two and we're fifty-fifty with everything. Do we"?

I processed this information for a moment or two then I said, "Why can't this be an opportunity for both of us? We go fifty-fifty with those guys; you go to Little Rock and run the station and I'll stay here and work these properties."

Kerby offered no resistance to this idea. "OK. I'll run it by them and see what they have to say."

Long and Atchley agreed.

I would be keeping my partner and, with regard to our growth, our efforts would be much more efficient.

A new company was formed and the four of us bought the station.

A Rough Spot Or Two

Purchase price of the station was $712,500.00. Each partner would own one-quarter of the company stock.

Long had the necessary cash and I suppose Atchley had his required portion on hand, but Kerby and I had used much of our cash reserve for our recent acquisitions so we were unable to contribute the full amount of our required cash contribution.

Long agreed to make up the difference, giving Kerby and I a period of time to come up with the remainder. The kicker was this: Long and Atchley would own fifty-one percent of the stock until such time as Kerby and I could repay Long the amount of our 'shortfall.'

When that cash was forthcoming the stock would be readjusted to reflect four owners of twenty-five percent each.

(To me, Long only agreed to do this because he saw Kerby's participation [and brilliance] as 'key' to making the project a success. There can be no other reason.)

Kerb and I thought that was fair. A contract was drawn and signed and we purchased KXXA-FM.

A Legendary Station Is Born

KXXA was licensed as a full Class-C FM, able to hang its antenna at 2,000 feet HAAT and broadcast with 100 kw. At the time the station antenna was on a shorter tower, but an application for a technical upgrade was perking at the FCC.

The upgrade would enable the station to relocate its tower to a spot on Shinall Mountain west of Little Rock. The antenna would hang at 1,663 feet HAAT!

Can you say 'Flame Thrower'? How about 'FLAME THROWER'?

Owned by local businessman Joe Mullen, KXXA was 'strategically' positioned in an All Business News format. It had a one-share of the audience and was doing very little business.

We saw the format hole as 'Country Music', a niche that was currently occupied by one AM station in the market.

Mr. Opporknockity was tuned up and hammering on the door.

Note: This was at the very beginning of the time when 'Country' was surging to the top of radio ratings all over the country. Timing is everything, right?

OK - So we're going Country. What'll we call the station? How will we roll it out?

The Call Letter Search

With but a few exceptions, call letters for radio stations located west of the Mississippi River begin with 'K'. Stations east of the river begin with 'W'. The FCC had a master list of available call letters from which broadcasters could choose. Kerby began his meticulous search.

He landed on a set of sensational call letters that did not show up on the 'available' list, but were also not found in the database that listed all commercial broadcast stations by call letters.

A mystery to be sure.

Enter Jason Shrinsky, the 'Sherlock Holmes' of FCC lawyers. In a conversation with Shrinsky, Kerby asked how this could be so.

Jason suggested a search of call letters assigned to Navy ships.

Voila!

The search revealed that the calls Kerby wanted – KSSN – had long been assigned to a now-mothballed Navy ship.

Jason initiated a conversation with the Department of the Navy which included a 'suggested' set of call letters for them should they agree to give up KSSN.

They agreed.

'96 KISSIN' was born!

A Trip To The Top

In order to prepare for a proper rocket launch of *96 KISSIN,'* Kerby moved to Little Rock in late August of 1978.

As it turned out, closing on the station did not occur until February of 1979, coinciding with the signing of a contract to purchase the market's leading AM station, KRLA (more on this to follow).

BOOM!

To say that KSSN was a success would be like saying Tom Brady is "a pretty good NFL quarterback" or that Tiger Woods "plays a decent game of golf."

When Kerby took over KXXA in February of 1979 the station was languishing in the ratings, and doing less than $250,000.00 in annual revenue.

A few months later the first Arbitron Ratings showed KSSN with a 6 share. Six months later it was a 12 share, and six months after that a 16 share. KSSN had gone from last to first in 18 months and was on track to produce annual revenue over two million dollars.

That growth continued for many more years.

Surprise, Surprise

Toward the end of 1980, with KSSN posting unheard-of revenue increases every month, Jim Long announced that he was pulling the plug on our deal because (paraphrasing) "Kerby's performance is not up to expectations."

No expectation of any kind was included in the contract we'd all signed and besides, Kerby was doing a fantastic job. But there it was: 'I'm kicking you out because...well...because I want to'.

Stunning.

We called Jason Shrinsky to discuss. He immediately morphed into his 'I can fix this' mode.

"Let me make a call. I'll get back to you."

The next thing we knew we were a). being represented by the finest business lawyer in Dallas, the attorney who, when an envelope with his name on the front lands on the desk of a potential litigant that litigant goes into apoplectic shock, and b). talking to a New York banker that Jason recommended.

Jason's comment? "Trust me. This will definitely get Long's attention."

Did.

The banker was Alan Griffith of The Bank Of New York, one of the few bankers of that day who viewed radio broadcasting as a solid business. We met with Alan who arranged a loan for us, enabling us to make up our 'shortfall' with Long. Within a week the stock was re-balanced – four partners @ 25% each...

...and Kerb continued to 'knock it outta the park' in Little Rock.

Note: Long could not have found a better operating partner for KSSN if he'd searched the world over - and back. He just needed someone to 'splain it to him!

Really...Politics?

Kerby was not a guy who spent a lot of time talking politics. He certainly was not uninformed...just uninterested I guess. *(By contrast, I'm probably too interested!)*

Anyway, one nice September day in 1979 we were talking business on the phone and as the conversation was about to end he said, "Paul, we have a guy in Little Rock who's going to be President of the United States someday."

"Who"? sez I, incredulously.

"Bill Clinton."

"Who he"?

"He's the governor of Arkansas."

"Of Arkansas"? I said. "No way a governor of Arkansas can be elected President. The state's too small to provide him with a political base and too southern to matter. Never happen."

"Oh yeah? Well let me tell you something. In spite of the fact that the *Arkansas Democrat* newspaper prints story after story about him chasing every skirt in the state, the folks down here think he hung the moon. I'm telling you...he's going to be President."

I shot back with, "Tell ya what. If he's ever elected President I'll buy you and your wife dinner at your favorite restaurant."

A few years later the four of us enjoyed dinner and drinks...on me...

...at Tio Pepe in Baltimore.

It's on Franklin Street.

Yum!

CHAPTER 10
IMPOSSIBLE

In January of 1979 we learned that KRLA-AM, Little Rock's leading AM station, was for sale. We were already scheduled to be in Little Rock in February to close on KSSN so we arranged for a meeting with Mr. Leonard Coe, KRLA's owner.

The Deal

At that time, radio stations were trading in multiples of seven to ten-times cash flow. KRLA had one million dollars in gross revenue and three hundred thousand dollars of operating cash-flow. A purchase price of $2.5 million dollars was agreed upon and a Letter of Intent was drawn up and signed.

In 1979 the wait time between the FCC filing of the application to transfer control of KRLA's license, and the Commission's grant of the application, was anywhere from four to six months. As such, our agreement included a Material Adverse Change clause (MAC) – a promise to the buyer whereby the seller guarantees the business will, at closing, be substantially as it was on the day the contract was signed.

There was also a Specific Performance clause requiring the buyer to appear with the money at the agreed upon closing date and time, and close the deal – a guarantee to the Seller.

The contract specified that the buyer put $250,000.00 in escrow, which we did.

Mr. Leonard Coe

KRLA was owned by Mr. Leonard Coe, a very fine 70-year old man who was much revered in Arkansas. Mr. Coe was indeed a Southern Gentleman.

As our meeting was wrapping up Mr. Coe looked at the four of us and said, “Ahm goin’ up tah Hot Spranghs tamarrah foah a day at thuh races. Would y’all like ta joihn me”?

My partners were uninterested.

I (a lover of Thoroughbred racing) immediately accepted his kind invitation.

“Fahn Pahul. Ah’ll pick ya up ‘roud nahn thutty. Ah’ll ask yew ta drahve and take mah bets ta the windahs. The rest of the day is ohn me.”

The next morning I slipped behind the wheel of Mr. Coe’s Caddilac and drove us to Hot Springs…in the pouring rain.

The track was muddy. It quickly became obvious that the horses Mr. Coe was betting on were not ‘mudders’.

He was having a very bad day at the windows.

Lunch was great. Our handicapping discussions were a blast. The conversation up and back was fascinating. All in all a wonderful day for me.

This was to be the only conversation I would have with Mr. Coe. He passed away a few months later.

His death triggered a set of ‘not to be believed’ events. Please read on.

Enter Toby

Shortly after Mr. Coe died his son, Toby, became the manager of the station.

At the time, we were told that Toby had been living in California where he had been engaged in writing songs. I was uncertain of the veracity of this information.

What was I *certain* of? If this information was true then Toby could not possibly possess the background or experience necessary to step in and manage a radio station with over $1million in gross revenue.

Nevertheless, there he was.

Mr. Coe's passing would turn out to be a station-changing event. In the meantime we were experiencing an unanticipated delay at the FCC.

I don't remember all of the details but the grant of our application was being delayed while Jim Long worked out some sort of unrelated but annoying business mess that (I believe) involved the SEC.

If I wanted to name horses after these two events I would have called one horse 'Toby's Arrival' and the other 'Long Delay'. In racing parlance these horses combined to form the perfect nega-xacta.

Under Toby's management, in a relatively short time the station's revenue began to dwindle, and by the time Long got his mess straightened out and it was time for us to close (late 1980) KRLA was out of compliance with the MAC clause.

For this reason we informed them that we did not intend to close the deal and we asked that they please return our escrow.

They refused and sued us for Specific Performance.

The Basics

Under Toby's guidance the stations were now on track to produce $750,000.00 in gross revenue and $100,000.00 in

Operating Cash Flow. Both numbers were far below what we'd been promised.

Based upon this material adverse change we counter-sued for return of escrow.

"Rose Law Firm. May I Help You"

I believe it was Shrinsky who suggested that we employ the Rose Law Firm, reputedly the best law firm in Arkansas.

We contacted them and in short order were working with two of their top lawyers.

Vincent W. Foster, Jr., Esq. (yes...*that* Vince Foster) would be the Lead Lawyer (called *First Chair)...*

...and Hillary Rodham Clinton, Esq. (yes...*that* Hillary Clinton) would be *Second Chair.*

(Can you dig it?)

We would be opposed by the venerable C. Alston Jennings, Sr., Esq., another of Little Rock's finest barristers.

Sidebar: It took quite a while to get all of this ready for the trial, which finally took place in mid-1981. I'll never forget Barbie and me flying to Little Rock for a deposition when the pilot came on the PA system to announce that President Reagan had been shot. It was March 31, 1981, our son Paul's twentieth birthday.

"All Rise"

Sometime in late summer/early fall the trial got underway, starting with the selection of the jury. I learned a lot from watching this process.

A 'jury of your peers' is one of the most important 'peer groups' we routinely select in America (*a 'peer group' being defined as "a group of people of approximately the same age, status, and interests").* One never knows what to expect from a randomly-chosen group of citizens selected for jury duty.

With an eye toward empaneling a jury that might favor his side, each lawyer gets to question potential jurors, accepting those he thinks are qualified and striking others. This goes back and forth until the lawyers have agreed on twelve people who will serve as jurors, and two alternates.

As one of the defendants in the case, I was hoping the lawyers would find several folks from this pool of potential jurors who would be able to get their arms around the discussion of things like 'material adverse change' and 'specific performance'. From the responses of the candidates I was becoming less and less convinced that this could be so.

By observation it was clear to me that members of the jury pool were largely not, per se, "a group of people of approximately the same age, status, and interests" as that of we defendants – a quartet of forty-something businessmen (three of whom were Yankees) all of whom were dressed in three-piece suits and sitting in a courtroom in Little Rock, Arkansas.

This 'pool' also featured a large selection of empty seats which I assumed were 'unoccupied' by busier people who'd found various and sundry ways of getting out of jury duty.

During jury selection there appeared a potential juror who was the owner of a store where he sold musical instruments and all accoutrements related thereto: reeds, strings, sheet music, et al.

Had I been the plaintiff's attorney I would have used one of my peremptory challenges to prevent this person from serving on the jury.

I was not.

He did not.

This gentleman was selected to serve on the jury, which to me was a game changer. A "whew" if you will.

Ten Days in Little Rock

The judge hammered the gavel and we were underway.

The four of us—Atchley, Confer, Long and Rothfuss—sat on the bench behind our Defense Counsel's table, where reposed the aforementioned Mr. Foster and Ms. Clinton. The elegant white-haired C. Alston Jennings, Sr. gave the opening statement for the prosecution.

Mr. Jennings was masterful indeed, the epitome of my (perhaps) pre-conceived notion of what to expect from a true Southern Gentleman Lawyer. So much so that in the middle of Mr. Jennings' opening statement I leaned over and whispered to Kerby, "I wish he was representing us."

Next, Vince Foster gave our opening statement and he, too, was masterful. Very straightforward and matter of fact.

I was completely reassured.

Early in the proceeding we learned that the music store owner had been elected Jury Foreman. I took this as a sign that the other jurors, with perhaps less business background, were comforted to know they had among them a compadre who could answer their questions in the privacy of the jury room.

The Genius And The Blackboard

On the morning of Day Three, Vince Foster entered the courtroom wheeling a portable four-by-five foot blackboard...chalk and all.

On the blackboard he wrote:

$1,000,000.00 — $750,000.00
$300,000.00 —— $100,000.00

Upon his arrival in courtroom and seeing the blackboard, Mr. Jennings grabbed some sort of cloth and wiped Vince's numbers off the board. But there was a problem. Because the cloth was dry it left a 'shadow' of the numbers still visible on the board.

This scenario was repeated every day. Numbers on. Numbers wiped off.

As the trial continued, each time Vince made reference to 'material adverse change' (the heart of the lawsuit) he'd go to the board and point to the numbers.

"Revenue down from one million dollars to seven hundred fifty thousand dollars.

"Cash flow down from three hundred thousand dollars to one hundred thousand dollars."

(Chalk shadow remaining.)

Benefit? Us.

Note: Could it be possible that Mr. Jennings didn't know that a wet cloth was required in order to remove all traces of those numbers?

And you say?

"I swear..."

I never worked at KSSN so I had very little first-hand knowledge of the 'day-to-day' of the stations. As a result, my time on the witness stand was limited to Q & A about station valuation, radio revenue and operating cash flow. The same was true for Jim and Jerry.

Because he'd served as GM of KSSN for over two years, Kerby spent more time on the stand than the other three of us combined.

One of our expert witnesses was Dick Kozacko, a broadcast broker who'd handled dozens of these transactions, nearly all of which were based upon multiples of operating cash flow.

As each day passed I believed more and more that there was no way we could be losing 'on the merits'. Citing the stellar reputation of Mr. Leonard Coe as the 'unknown factor', Vince was...well...he was unconvinced (pun intended).

Crunch Time

As the final witness for the prosecution, Mr. Jennings called Toby Coe to the stand. He chose to make Toby's testimony mostly about his father...how Mr. Leonard Coe was a Little Rock icon, a great and charitable man who ran a great radio station.

"...and these boys came down here and used KSSN to drive down Mr. Leonard Coe's business with the hope of getting his station for a lower price."

(Whaaat?)

But now it was Vince's turn to shine.

Short version: After ten minutes of 'back and forth' with Toby, Vince went to the blackboard and 'chalked up' the numbers. Large...really Large.

Here's a summary of the 'home run' closing Q & A between Vince Foster and Toby Coe.

Foster: "So, Mr. Coe...would you say the difference between one million dollars and seven hundred fifty thousand dollars is material"?

Coe: "Mmmm, noo."

Foster: "Really? Well let me ask you this...would you say the difference between three hundred thousand dollars of profit and one hundred thousand dollars of profit is...adverse"?

Coe: (a pause...then a blurt) - "Well...it isn't very good."

Foster: "Thank you Mr. Coe. No further questions."

The Verdict

We won the case.

Vince Foster handled this case beautifully. Having the music store owner as the Jury Foreman was (I believe) a big advantage for us, again, because he could speak to his fellow jurors on business-related questions and practices with knowledge and authority.

Retrospectives

#1. This trial should never have happened. All we wanted was a return of our escrow based on an obvious condition of the contract. (BTW – The court also awarded us half of our attorney fees.)

#2. We had several lunches and dinners with our lawyers. Vince Foster was a great lawyer and a great guy.

When I tell folks this tale of having worked with Vince Foster, many ask if I believe he took his own life. Sadly, I believe he did. Here's why:

I believe Vince never wanted to be in Washington, but because one of his best friends had been elected President and asked him to come to Washington and be his White House Chief of Staff, Vince capitulated. *You simply cannot say 'no' to the President of the United States,* he might have thought.

Shortly after arriving in D. C. all manner of 'potentially bad for the Clintons' stuff began to erupt: Whitewater, Hillary's cattle investment, Travelgate, Bill's peccadilloes. Just to name a few.

I believe Vince Foster knew a lot about all of this stuff, and saw a strong possibility that, if there were ever court proceedings or Congressional hearings, he'd be required to place his hand on the Bible and swear to tell the truth – some of which may have had the effect of throwing his best friend (who also happened to be the POTUS) under the bus.

I think the pressure got to him and he saw no other way out. Just my thoughts.

Though I cannot say 'I knew him well' I will always harbor wonderful memories of Vincent W. Foster, Jr., Esq., and the terrific work he did for us.

#3. Hillary had a helluva time keeping four early-forties Type-A personalities focused and under control.

Example: For me, sitting there for hours each day was boredom to the max.

The Oak Ridge Boys were riding high on the charts with 'Elvira'.

One mid-morning, with Jerry Atchley sitting next to me and the trial droning on, I decided (quietly) to lighten things up a bit. I leaned over, and in the rhythm of the song I whispered in Atchley's ear, 'El-Vire- Ah'.

At this Jerry grinned and began to silently 'mouth' the lyrics as we both began a nearly-imperceptible left-to-right 'sway'- in the rhythm of the song.

We were a duet - both of us nearly motionless but nevertheless 'swaying'...and silently (or so we believed) mouthing, 'El-Vire-Ah...El-Vire-Ah. My heart's...on fire-ah...for El-Vire-Ah'.

Hillary turned in her chair and gave us a stare unlike any I'd ever seen before. Or (thankfully) since. How she detected our misdeed I'll never know. A sixth sense?

She ... was ... furious!

No. She was livid!

We stopped our 'act' immediately.

(Thank God she got to us before we reached the 'Giddey-up, Um-papa, Um-papa Mau Mau' part or we'd certainly have been cited for contempt of court.)

On the way to lunch and just outside the restaurant we received a serious blast of Hillary Wrath. She read us the Riot Act - a 'stream-of-consciousness diatribe' laced with words I'd previously believed were known only to sailors. A tongue-lashing that we richly deserved.

To be fair, Hillary *was* representing us in a $2.5 million dollar legal case.

Needless to say, after this episode we were on our very best behavior.

(Since that day I've often wondered what it might have been like for Bill anytime Hillary got seriously p-o'd. Whoa Nellie!)

#4. Because the trial took place during a time between Bill Clinton's terms as Governor of Arkansas we never got to meet him. Later, Jerry became close friends with the Clintons.

CHAPTER 11
SELL THE BABY

So...it's mid-1979.

At that time FCC rules imposed limits on the number of radio stations any one company could own – fourteen stations, seven AM and seven FM...in any configuration that added to fourteen. You could own an AM/FM combo in seven markets, or an AM here and an FM there with a combo or two somewhere else...all adding to fourteen. You get the picture.

Kerby and I had a stated goal: To accumulate seven dynamite AM/FM combos in small markets and own them forever.

In the latter part of 1980 I got a call from our favorite broker, Dick Kozacko, a call that, in no uncertain terms, really tipped that apple cart.

"Hey Richard," sez I, "Whatcha gonna sell us today"?

But this was not a 'sell *you* something' call.

Kozacko: "Would you be interested in selling Williamsport"?

Wow!

A thought that had never crossed our minds.

My mind was racing.

(Sell WLYC and WILQ? Our Baby? I don't think so. Maybe. Not a chance. Why do you ask?)

"Geez Dick...ahmmm, who wants to know"?

"Confidentially of course, but we got a call from the attorney representing the *Grit* newspaper. You know these folks. The family has published their Sunday-only newspaper for many, many decades, right there in Williamsport. It's distributed all over America.

"Anyway, a few years ago they purchased some TV stations and now they want to get into radio. "So, what do you think"?

I told Dick I'd talk with Kerby and get back to him.

Dick said, "I think I can get you at least $2 million for the stations."

(Smelling salts please!)

I was surprised when Kerby opined, "Well, we have nothing to lose by having a conversation."

I called Dick and told him we'd be willing to discuss the matter.

We got a Confidentiality Agreement signed and over the next few weeks we exchanged some documents and conversation.

They gave us an offer of $2,150,000.00.

We kicked it around for a few days and, because we had nothing on the horizon to replace these stations, decided against moving forward.

We politely declined.

It's A Funny Thing...

It's now January of 1981.

Kerb is on the phone with an opportunity.

"WGXL is a full Class C FM for sale in Laurens, South Carolina. The station antenna is on a short stick (radio tower) but there's an application on file with the FCC to build 1,400 feet of steel and throw a primary signal over Greenville-Spartanburg-Anderson (*a strip market*). This new huge footprint presents a great opportunity for us. We should go for it!" (*I believe the purchase price was $750,000.00 – not sure.)*

NOTE: At that time the FCC license of a Class C FM allowed for the station antenna to hang at 2,000 feet HAAT and broadcast with 100-kw (100,000 watts). As you will learn: 'Underdeveloped Class C FMs' would soon be providing us with magnificent opportunities.

Kerby had gathered a ton of information about this large 'strip market'. We went over it with a fine-tooth comb.

Our conclusion? *We gotta get this station.*

But howinthehell can we pay for it?

Ahmmm...sell WLYC/WILQ?

I called Kozacko.

Short version: We re-opened talks with *Grit* and negotiated an Asset Purchase Agreement. The purchase price was $2,100,000.00. Part of the Agreement called for me to stay and run the stations for a period of two years.

(*I believed this was unnecessary and an extra cost that Grit should not have to bear. I'd developed a team of 'managers-to-be'- two terrific young broadcaster-businessmen, Warren Diggins and Dave Banks, who were totally ready to take over the reins. Grit would have none of it.*)

Kerb and I talked it over. Because we still owned the Reading and Cortland stations with no prospects to sell either, and because *Grit* understood that I had obligations to look after those stations as well (and agreed to allow me to do so) we agreed to their terms.

I would stay in Williamsport for two years. Kerby would continue to manage KSSN and look after our new Greenville acquisition. That was the plan.

We transferred ownership to *Grit* in the summer of 1981.

As you will see, Kerby and I went on to own and develop many radio stations and work with scores of really excellent people, in large markets and small. At no time, however, would I have a radio station with a staff that exceeded the loyalty, attitude, or accomplishments of the staff of these two radio stations in tiny Williamsport, Pennsylvania. These people were Tops!

Note: This sale was bittersweet for me. Over the previous six years I'd had the pleasure of working with a group of outstanding colleagues – ambitious, talented, goal-oriented young broadcast professionals who 'left it all on the field' every day. Many of these former colleagues have stayed in touch with me for all these years. I am grateful and humbled.

Palmetto State Radio

WGXL was owned by Monte Dupuy and Gene Phillips. Monte was a well-known TV personality and Gene a Media Rep.

We hired a top Greenville Attorney to do the contract work for us. As radio station transactions go, this one went off without a hitch.

WSSL

We decided to go with the 'Three-In-A-Row' Country Music format that had been so successful for us in Little Rock.

A repeat of his KSSN coup found Kerby coming up with our new call letters - 'WSSL'. We said 'Hello' to 'Whistle One-Hundred'.

And we needed a General Manager.

Recall that Dave Bernstein was our Sales Manager at WHUM in Reading, PA. We asked Dave to be our partner and serve as the GM of WSSL, which he agreed to do.

A Different Direction

A pattern was emerging.

Back when we bought WKRT-AM/FM in Cortland, NY, the FM (a full Class B facility) had been simulcasting its AM sister-stations' programming. The station was also eligible to change its antenna height and provide signal coverage to Ithaca. In combination with a format change on the FM, this doubled the size of the available listening audience as well as the number of potential advertising clients.

KXXA-FM in Little Rock, AR (a full Class C facility - soon to be KSSN) had been broadcasting business news. The station was also eligible to double its HAAT by changing antenna locations, thus doubling its footprint and adding another thirty percent to its total available audience.

In front of us now was WGXL (soon to be WSSL), licensed to Laurens, SC, yet another full Class C facility with an antenna hanging on a short stick, but with a construction permit to build 1,400 feet of steel closer to Greenville; thereby tripling the footprint and adding countless potential listeners and clients.

Hmmm.

Note: At this time, Kerby and I were not researching markets specifically to find underdeveloped FM radio stations for sale. We had no idea that we'd soon have top-notch Broadcast Brokers doing exactly that for us!

WSSL Redux

Dave Bernstein's agreement to take the reins in Greenville posed a real problem for us. First off, WHUM was a stand-alone AM station at a time when FM was gaining on AM with every stride. Also, to be candid, the management team that we'd forced into co-existence in Reading wasn't really very...'teamy' – if you catch my drift.

Oh hell! Might as well say it.

Messrs Bernstein and Kirk weren't getting along. What was worse was Dave (Sales Guru) was about to depart, and Henry was making loud noises about being 'a full 1/3 partner' when we bought our next station.

(To which we replied, "Good with us. Next time just throw in one-third of the money and you're in." Henry did not receive this news very well at all. Next thing we knew Henry was coming to us to partner with him in a Burger King Restaurant in Dallas, TX. He had the money necessary to be a 1/3 owner and said he'd go to Texas and run the show. We said 'OK' and that's what he did. This ended up in the Top Three of the worst decisions I ever made - another story for another time.)

Given the harsh cold winds swirling around stand-alone AM stations in general and WHUM in particular, we listed the station for sale. Much to my surprise we signed a contract in no time at all. I don't remember the sale price but I do note that a). WHUM was in the black, b). we sold it for more than we paid, and c). we were sooo happy to get out of there with bank accounts intact.

No more stand-alone AMs for us.

WSSL Performance

We built the new tower, we changed the format to Three-In-A-Row Country and the call letters to 'WSSL – WHISTLE 100'. By 1984 our gross revenue was in excess of $2,000,000.00.

Concert patches from some favorite WSSL concert promotions.

Cost to construct the 1,400-foot tower was right at one million dollars. Watching it go up was astonishing. If you've been 'up close' with a tall FM tower you must know that these guys who climb around @ 1,000 feet above ground putting steel together...must be out of their cotton-picking minds! It's why in 1981 they were paid upwards of $50/hour!

We hung the antenna and turned on the flame-thrower. The bad news: The ascending terrain from the antenna location to the City of Greenville prevented the signal from being 'fabulous' in the southernmost part of the city. North of the city it boomed - all the way to the foothills of the Piedmont.

The great news: In Spartanburg and Anderson the signal was so strong you could get it on the rims of your glasses! After six months of a very bumpy start-up we decided to 'forget Greenville' and concentrate our efforts in places where we could actually be heard.

Success was ours!

WSSL remains a top-rated Country station to this day.

CHAPTER 12
JACKSON…IN A FEVER

In early 1981, Kerby returned a phone call to Joe Mullen (from whom we purchased KSSN). Joe told Kerby about the availability of an AM/FM combo in Jackson, Mississippi.

WJDX was Jackson's leading AM station, broadcasting news and MOR (middle of the road) music. WZZQ-FM, another full Class C, was in a rock format and knockin' 'em dead with men aged 18 to 44.

The stations were owned by Lamar Life Broadcasting, Inc., ("LLB") a subsidiary of the Lamar Life Insurance Company.

Joe gave Kerby some solid information about station ratings and financials, which Kerby related to me. Man, it was easy to see that 'this one was for us'!

Oddly the seller required a stock sale, a non-negotiable condition if a contract was to be agreed upon. Combined billing of the two radio stations was $1.4 million with OCF (Operating Cash Flow) of about $350,000.00.

(For tax reasons we always insisted on purchasing assets. In an asset sale the buyer purchases only the assets of the company – furniture, fixtures and equipment, buildings, vehicles, land, licenses, existing contracts, etc. Using the purchase price of the assets as his basis, the buyer then writes up the value of the assets for purposes of depreciation—a huge tax advantage. In a stock deal the buyer gets the company 'intact and as is', i.e. all of the aforementioned assets and all of the liabilities. All the 'happy', all the 'sad'…and everything in-between. In a stock sale the only difference between the 'before' and the 'after' is the names of the

stockholders. The 'sad' is solidly in play if the company's assets were written off prior to the stock sale.)

"Asking price for the stations is $4.5 million dollars."

(Wow! Thirteen times cash flow? Really?)

But Wait...There's More

When we expressed our surprise at the asking price, Joe Mullen went on to explain that the company owned a 'note-payable' for $2.5 million dollars that was amortizing at a rate of about $25,000.00 per month. The buyer of the stock of LLB would receive this note. (If memory serves, Lamar was valuing the stations at $3 million and the note at $2.5 million.)

The Story Behind the Note

Lamar Life Broadcasting had at one time been the licensee of a Jackson TV station, WLBT, Channel 3. During the civil rights movement of the late '50s and '60s the station took editorial positions that were offensive to many groups that supported the movement. When it became time for the station to file the application for license renewal these groups filed Petitions to Deny the renewal with the Federal Communications Commission (FCC).

This battle went back and forth in the courts for over ten years, finally ending with the FCC denying LLB's license renewal, and instead awarding it to a coalition of the protesting groups.

While the law afforded the FCC the power to award the license in this manner, the Commission had no claim whatsoever on the assets of LLB. Needing to own these assets in order to be a viable business (TV stations need cameras, towers, studios, etc.) the new licensee negotiated a deal with LLB to acquire these assets for approximately $2.5 million, a deal that closed in late 1981.

Details of this fascinating history are available on Wikipedia.

https://en.wikipedia.org/wiki/WLBT

Oh yeah, I almost forgot. There was no Country music on FM in Jackson.

All Dressed Up And No Cash To Go

This was a whale of an opportunity but we didn't have the money.

"When the student is ready the teacher will appear." This admonition has been attributed to Siddhartha Guatama Shakyamuni (among others). Its eternal truth was about to be upon us.

Enter Shrinsky

Nearly every week it was routine for us to have conversations with our esteemed FCC Counsel, Jason Shrinsky, thus he was always up to date with the status of our various companies.

A call during this particular week ended with Jason asking, "So what else is up"? Kerby launched into the tale of Jackson, explaining the details of the deal and lamenting the fact that, while this was right up our alley we had no money to pursue the deal.

Jason said, "Money? You're worried about money? The bigger concerns for you guys should be a). do you have the time to devote to another property at this time, and b). do you have the talent to make it work.

"Do you"?

"Because if money is your problem...you *have* no problem. That can be remedied in short order."

(Paul/Kerby Chorus: "Huh"?)

Jason told us about TA Associates, a very successful venture capital firm in Boston with a keen interest in broadcast investing.

"I'll call them and get you started."

Note: While we had no way of knowing this at the time, thanks to Jason Shrinsky this conversation and our meeting with TA Associates would be the catalyst for what we were soon to accomplish. Jason was a great communications lawyer who also understood the radio business. He was and is an even better friend. Exactly how great? At that time many law offices specializing in communications issues were located on DeSales Street in downtown Washington DC. Some fellow lawyers and 'in the know' broadcasters referred to Jason Shrinsky as 'The Wizard of DeSales Street'.

A Giant Step Forward

Shortly thereafter, armed with our career histories, details of the deals we'd done, and the financial statements (proof of performance) of the various stations we'd owned, Kerby and I were off to Boston and the offices of TA Associates.

In the paneled conference room we met with a group of sophisticated financial gurus (most with MBAs), men our age whose representation of multiple wealthy corporations and individuals included the investing of tens of millions of client dollars in entrepreneurial companies, in exchange for pieces of those companies.

For the next couple of hours we regaled them with our story. How at age eighteen Kerby and I had made a vow to someday own a radio station together, then went from this station to that, sometimes working together, sometimes not; from Williamsport in 1958 to Baltimore in 1963 to management in Annapolis in the early seventies.

And then, in 1975, going 'all in' to buy our first stations.

We showed them the fantastic revenue growth we'd created in Williamsport, Reading (not fantastic, but pretty good), Cortland, and Little Rock, AR, and we told them we'd sold Williamsport, Reading and Cortland, all for a profit, and bought WSSL in Greenville, SC.

And we'd done all this with our own money.

They asked tons of questions, most of which began with "how" and "why."

The meeting ended with a handshake and a promise from TA to have contracts for us in a day or two. Oh...and their assurance that they'd back the Jackson deal.

Our TA contact would be Richard Churchill, a young man who quickly 'got' the radio business and, more importantly, mastered the parameters of what were (and weren't) good deals. He was a great teammate.

From their questions and comments it was evident that they'd done a lot of homework on us, and I'm sure that Jason's strong advocacy on our behalf went a long way toward achieving this result. We would also learn later that TA viewed the Jackson deal as a 'no-brainer' because of the existence of the $2.5 million dollar note-receivable.

Plus our stories had them in stitches. The 'stories' were our history. To me telling them was kinda like doing my radio show 'live'. I was thrilled. Imagine, a couple of fresh-faced

Pennsylvania German boys come to Boston and leave with a huge deal. Yesssss!

Note: Here's the breakdown of our deal with TA. They would arrange for and guarantee all bank loans. They would contribute cash equity equal to ten or fifteen percent of the purchase price. In exchange, TA would receive one-third of the equity. For our share of the equity (one-third each) Kerby and I would both be required to contribute twenty-five thousand dollars in cash per deal.

We took the folks at TA at their word and entered negotiations with Mike McRee, President of Lamar Life Broadcasting. Supported by a letter from TA assuring LLB that we had the money, our talks went smoothly. By May we had signed a contract and filed the application with the FCC.

Sidebar: By 1990 the best deal a radio entrepreneur could get from the venture firms was fifteen, maybe twenty percent of the equity, with the venture firm retaining the rest. How times changed!

The Dynamic Duo

The greatest and most important assets any radio station can ever have are its FCC license (no license, no station) and its staff.

Consider that, not counting land or buildings, if a radio station goes broke and they must 'sheriff's sale' the assets they'll be lucky to get $200,000.00. No one wants to buy used radio equipment. Why then do (did) companies pay millions of dollars for radio stations?

First of all, scarcity. At that time there were far fewer commercial radio stations on the air, not many of which were 'large footprint' stations.

You'll recall that radio stations are valued based upon multiples of Operating Cash Flow, otherwise called 'profit'. So how is said profit created?

It is created by great people with great ideas who provide great programming, outstanding community involvement and service, and exemplary attention to the needs of their clients and listeners. To produce maximum profit you must first have great people.

When we bought the LLB stations we got two 'large footprint' radio facilities and a basketful of 'large footprint' folks. What a staff!

Hotter Than A Pepper Sprout

The management team was sensational.

The General Manager was Marshall Magee…the Sales Manager, Kenny Windham.

I could do three paragraphs on these guys and never run out of praise. In the interest of brevity try this: "Marshall and Kenny were as good as it ever gets." So good that starting Day One we realized the best thing we could do was feed them great ideas, then get out of the way and watch their brilliance.

The best news was that both men had outstanding people skills, which is why top to bottom the staff was terrific.

Change Gotta Come

WJDX needed no tinkering whatsoever.

However, we saw WZZQ in a Rock format as 'self-limited'. Yes...it was rated #1 with Men 18–44, which was nice, but that's not the 'money demographic' needed if a station is to be a drop-dead hit.

On the other hand, a Country Music format would skew about 60% men and 40% women, all adults 25–54, which advertisers of all stripes would love.

Ta Daaa! There was no Country on the FM band in Jackson, a market that mirrored Little Rock.

Hmmm.

We decided we'd change the format to Country when we got the stations, probably in September or October.

We selected WMSI as the new call letters. "MISS 103, The Station Of The State."

Oh Oh!

In early June we heard a rumor that another Class C FM in the market was planning to change their format to Country. Kerby and I always believed that 'who gets there first with the most, wins', so this was not good news – potentially a disaster.

We needed help...and fast.

The Big 'No-No' - Prior Control

FCC rules require the licensee of a radio station to be *in control* of that station right up to the minute the station changes hands, and especially during the 'wait time' between the filing of an application for transfer of control and the FCC grant of that application. Violation of this rule, called 'prior control', comes with serious penalties including voiding deals, disallowing future applications, etc.

All in all, not good for us because the only way to avoid this disaster would be to change the FM format ASAP, prior to the FCC grant. LLB could do this if they wanted to, but we could not be involved in the implementation of such a decision because even a *charge* of 'prior control' would likely delay the FCC grant, and put us on FCC radar when future applications are filed.

Or could we?

Suppose a radio station licensee signs a contract with a program consultant who is charged with recommending program additions and subtractions, personnel changes, logo and format changes and so on...and at some time during the life of the contract said consultant wants to buy the station. Would it be legal? Could it be done?

So long as it can be demonstrated that the licensee always retained the absolute right to accept or reject any and all of these recommendations...yes it would and yes it could.

Risky? You bet. And the legal 'fine line' would require extreme care and meticulous record-keeping.

It definitely is 'working the rules' but yes, it is doable. So sayeth Jason L. Shrinsky, Esq. In early June we approached Mike McRee.

We told Mike of our plans for WZZQ (we also told Marshall and Kenny), informed him of 'the rumor' and made him a proposition: you hire us as program consultants. Serving in that capacity we lay out the case for a format change on WZZQ that would necessitate a 're-imaging', a change of call letters, etc. Mike and LLB would be in charge of all decisions, which would be carefully documented.

Mike allowed as to how "Country on FM won't work in Jackson." Ulp! If we were to be successful in proving our case we'd have to show Mike the upside inherent in owning a #1-

rated Adults 25-54 station (Country or otherwise), as opposed to the limited revenue growth offered by a Rock station with a narrow audience demographic of Men 18-44.

For proof, we showed Mike the rating and revenue histories of WILQ and KSSN and tried to assure him that he'd suffer little if any drop in revenue from the time of this format change to the day of the closing, estimated to be October first.

"How 'bout it"?

Mike agreed to our plan. The man was a gamer!

Note: My bet is that Mike engaged in long conversations with Marshall and Kenny who assured him that our assessment of the situation was correct and the risk of revenue loss was minimal and very short-term.

Short version: There was a helluva lot to do. We got busy. Complete with a massive billboard campaign, MISS 103 was born around July 4th .

"ROCK AUDIENCE GOES CRAZY: BRINGS DOWN RADIO TOWER"

If WZZQ listeners had backed their threats with action, this would have been the banner headline in the *Jackson Clarion-Ledger* after we implemented the format change.

These folks were *furious.* For the next twenty days they melted our phone lines.

Day by day, little by little, the calls that were initially steeped in "You rotten $%&sa>#ches" were becoming "We really love the music on MISS 103."

Firstest With The Mostest

By the end of July and early August the rumor we'd been hearing became the reality. An FM competitor changed their format to Country.

Too late.

The first post-format-change ratings revealed MISS 103 with a nine share and the competitor with a two. We closed on the stations around October 1. The fall Arbitron (which came out in January) showed MISS 103 with a twelve-share of Adults 25-54, tied for #1.

In the next book we had a seventeen-share. MISS 103 was Jackson's #1 radio station. Marshall, Kenny and the outstanding staff turned this into huge revenue increases.

Performance

The FM format was changed to Country and the call letters to 'WMSI – The Station Of The State'. We didn't tamper with WJDX or the staff of either station. Combined revenue for 1982 was $1,485,000.00. By 1984 revenue was in excess of $2,630,000.00.

The early performance of MISS 103 solidified our position with TA Associates. Richard Churchill's ability to quickly assess the investment side of a radio broadcasting opportunity matched our ability to quickly assess the operational and competitive side, a combination that enabled us to get to (or get away from) deals much faster than other potential buyers. Which is why brokers often brought opportunities to us first. We were a great team.

Unlike TA in assessing this deal, Kerby and I made light of the Promissory Note we were about to acquire as part of the transaction. We knew nothing about the condition of the group guaranteeing the note, and were not about to spend time learning. We were laser-focused on building the business of the radio stations. "Maybe they'll pay this off, maybe they won't" was our attitude.

Some fifteen months after we bought the stations the note guarantors contacted us to inquire about the discount they could expect if they paid off the note early.

They were told that there'd be no discount.

They said 'OK'.

A few weeks later we received payment in full for the note...over $2-million dollars.

Ya gotta love stock deals!

CHAPTER 13
SOUTHERN COMFORT

In 1981 Kerby moved to West Lake, a beautiful subdivision west of Augusta, Georgia. "Easy access to oversee WSSL and a short plane hop to check on Little Rock, " sez he.

And as it turned out, Jackson, MS, too.

I was engaged in managing WLYC/WILQ for *Grit Publishing* while at the same time preparing to sell WHUM in Reading. The sale of Cortland would soon follow.

By this time Kerby had fallen in love with living in the south and was already prompting me with its virtues.

A Time Share At Hilton Head...And 'Finding Aiken'

Wealthy industrialists and businessmen discovered Aiken, South Carolina in the early nineteen-hundreds. The mild winter weather offered these folks enhanced winter living via a 'five-sport' opportunity: golf, tennis, horseback riding, hunting and fishing.

By the 1920s Aiken had also become an A#1 place to break and train young Thoroughbred horses. As a kid I remember my Dad talking about how he'd like to send some of his horses to Aiken someday. (He never did.)

In 1980 Barbie and I purchased a one week time share in a condo at Hilton Head Island, to be used during the first week in October. We were there in October of 1981 when Kerb called me and asked me to come to Augusta for a day of meetings.

To plan my trip I got a road map which revealed Aiken to be in the direct line between Hilton Head and Augusta. My curiosity made me take that route.

Beautiful

I arrived in Aiken and began driving aimlessly around, eventually stumbling onto South Boundary Avenue in 'the old section'. I thought I'd found paradise.

Beautiful old homes on large lots. Live oak trees provided superb canopies for the wide streets. Dripping with class and charm it was. In short, everything I'd ever imagined a fine southern town would be.

(I was thinking: We love old houses. Barbie would absolutely adore this. If we have to move down here I think Aiken is where we should live.)

At our meeting Kerby convinced me to move to Augusta. His argument?

"What we've seen with Little Rock and Jackson is but the tip of an iceberg. Our opportunity lies in this region. We work best when we're together. You gotta get yourself down here."

I drove back to Hilton Head and a few days later, while en route to Pennsylvania, I told Barbie I thought we'd need to move south in the next few months.

Whirlwind

Here's what happened in those next few months – abbreviated version.

I called Dick Kozacko and listed the Cortland stations for sale.

I began trying to convince the *Grit* folks that they no longer needed me...that Warren and Dave were past ready to take the reins and 'think of the money you'll save if you don't have to pay me a salary'. (By February they'd agreed.)

We put our house on the market.

Lemon Twiss'

February 27, 1982. Big wet snowflakes were falling like crazy when I left Williamsport for Augusta, GA. The roads were a sloppy mess and it wasn't long before my sliver and navy blue El Dorado was an all gray mess, totally covered with road salt residue. A few days later I was scheduled to meet Barbie and Peter (our youngest son) at the Augusta airport. The search for a house would begin the next day.

By the time I got to Harrisburg and I-81 the snow had lessened somewhat. As I crossed the Maryland/West Virginia line it stopped completely. I spent the night in a motel near Blacksburg, Virginia, arose early and headed for Georgia. I'll never forget 'topping the rise' on I-77 in southern Virginia around 8 AM. Starting down the mountain I saw a magnificent view of North Carolina. The temperature was 48 degrees.

(All I could think was, 'I'm gonna love this'.)

The car looked like hell – it was embarrassing. I made a vow to find a car wash as soon as I got to Augusta. ETA, Eleven AM.

Welcome To Augusta

Somehow I found myself downtown on Greene Street where I discovered a car wash – a really good car wash. The kind where you get out and watch while they make it look like new again. On the wall to the left of the entrance was the Main Menu, displaying the various levels and pricing of the car washes being offered.

I pulled up to the entrance where I was greeted by a crisply-dressed young black fellow, obviously The Man In Charge. He gave the car a thorough 'look-over' and as the window rolled down he said, “You, my friend, have come to *precisely* the right place. You are in *need* of a car wash...yes indeed.”

(His flawless presentation had me at ‘precisely’.)

“Yeah. I just drove through a snowstorm in Pennsylvania,” sez I. “Road salt.”

“Mmm Hmmm. Seen *that* before. May I suggest our Top-O-The-Line wash”?

“I was hoping you would.”

He laughed. “Right,” he said.

Then, referring to the selection of after-wash interior scents being offered, he asked, “...and what *flavor* would you like”?

(“Precisely”? “Flavor”? What a super cool dude. This was wonderful. I was having a blast. It was Georgie Goodman Redux. [see Alias Emperor Rodgers.]

“What flavors do you have,”? sez I.

“We have Lavender...New Car...Baby Powder.....and Lemon Twiss’.”

I said, “I think I’ll have the Lemon Twist.”

He pointed his index finger at me and said (approvingly), “Good choice.”

What a character!

And hey, they made my car look like new again.

Note: I made it a point to visit that car wash a few times but my 'newest best friend' was no longer there. He deserved to find greener pastures. I hope he did.

House-hunting - Monday March 1

A few days later Barbie, Peter and I were en route to Aiken for a 'look-around'. Barbie fell in love with Aiken, as I knew she would.

Kerby had hooked us up with an Augusta real estate agent who we met the next day. He showed us a couple of new-ish houses in Augusta. "Nice," we said. "But we want to live in Aiken."

The agent was unimpressed and insisted on showing us more Augusta properties. After a bit of a struggle he finally set us up for a meeting with an Aiken agent, Gayle Lofgren.

We told Gayle we wanted to see some of the older places. She took us to see 'Let's Pretend'. (Most of the cottages in the old section of Aiken had names.)

'Let's Petend's original structure was built in the late 1870s. An addition followed around 1890.

The good news: 'Let's Pretend' was beautiful and charming.

The bad news? 'Let's Pretend' needed complete renovation.

We bought it.

We sold our house. We sold the Cortland stations. We moved to Aiken in August of 1982.

Note: Gayle became a dear friend. This beautiful Southern lady introduced us to Wade and Sissy Brodie (another beautiful Southern lady) who took us under their wing and 'introduced us' to Aiken, which made our transition to the south as tasty as a fresh-baked pecan pie.

Living in Aiken, SC was one of the very best things that ever happened for Barbie and me. There was never one moment when we didn't feel completely welcomed there. The social life was indescribably wonderful. We love Aiken and our many friends who still reside there.

Note: Turns out Rudyard Kipling was once a guest at 'Let's Pretend'. (Quick joke follows: - Reggie: "Do you like Kipling"? Cedric: "I don't know Old Chap, I've never Kippled.")

Deals 'R Us

By this time we'd established a solid working relationship with several brokers, none more solid and enjoyable than that we enjoyed with the late Jay Bowles of Blackburn & Company.

Jay had been a sales rep for Associated Press, calling on radio stations to convince them to put AP services in their stations. Jay knew almost everybody in radio. We were about to become Jay's 'go-to' buyers.

WIGGLE 106

Next up was an opportunity to buy an AM/FM combo licensed to Orangeburg, SC, brought to us by Bob Marshall, another of Blackburn's fine brokers.

WPJS-FM (**W**e **P**roclaim **J**esus **S**aves) was an under-developed Class C FM in a Christian format. We were told that the station antenna could be moved some twenty miles north and throw a competitive signal over Columbia, the state capital of South Carolina. (The AM, WDIX, was dead-in-the-water. Great call letters. Little else to recommend.)

My recollection is that we paid $1.2 million for the stations.

Finding Tom Love

So...when searching for a General Manager for your radio station you place Classified Ads in the trade papers or contact headhunters, right?

Nope.

You get on an airplane where you hope your assigned seat will be next to a lady you've never met, one whose brother is in radio. You tell her that you're looking for a General Manager and she tells you her brother should be a candidate.

This is exactly how we found Tom Love, one of the two or three best GM's ever to join our company.

Kerby got on a plane and sat next to a young woman named Diane Love. At some point in their conversation Kerb mentioned that he was in the radio business. Diane told Kerby that her brother Tom was also – that he was in management at a station in Florida and was very successful.

When Kerby told Diane he was looking for a GM she suggested that he talk with her brother, and gave him Tom's number.

Kerby called Tom, after which conversation Kerby called to tell me he was going to meet with Tom, and if the meeting went well he might want to hire him.

I said, "If you believe he's the right person, go for it," which Kerby did.

Note: My first contact with Tom occurred on the day we closed on the radio stations. He was my partner before I met him.

This is a perfect example of how Kerby and I worked together - always with strong mutual trust in one another. No classified ad campaign or headhunter would ever have turned up anyone better than Tom...or even as good.

...And A Program Director

We also hoped to find a 'for-realsie' professional morning person who'd be willing to join us in little old Orangeburg, SC.

Tom outdid himself. He found Charlie Boswell.

As I recall, Charlie was working at a radio station in Charleston, SC. He was unhappy with the instability at this station and wanted a better opportunity.

One Sunday morning in early fall Barbie and I met Charlie and Martha (Mrs. Boswell) for lunch at a restaurant in Columbia, SC. Within ten minutes it was evident that Charlie 'knew his stuff', and was the person we needed to do mornings and be our Program Director.

We offered. Charlie accepted. The rest is history.

Charlie and Tom got WIGL off to a lightning-fast start, proving once again that where the radio business is concerned, other than a large footprint signal, the only other asset required for success is great people. In fact 'great people' is far and away the most important asset.

Ya Gotta Make It Wiggle

So...using our 'regular formula' (see KSSN, WSSL) we changed the call letters to WIGL ('WIGGLE 106'), reimaged the station, and changed the format to Country.

From its location fifty miles south of Columbia, WIGL covered a large number of rural counties, most of which had radio stations of their own. None of these stations sounded very good to me, especially those broadcasting Country music.

We covered the area with 'The Wiggle Worm' ...

... billboards and bumper stickers and all kinds of stuff.

WIGGLE 106 was an instant success.

Onward!

Shortly after the closing we filed our application to change the antenna location…

…which was denied!

Whaaa…?

What the H!!! Why?

Bureaucratic Baloney

The FCC had a rule that no two radio stations whose Post Offices were within ninety miles of one another could be owned by the same principals. As the crow flies, the Orangeburg, SC and Laurens, SC post offices were 88 miles apart.

A stupid rule but 'Application Denied' nonetheless.

WIGL was off to a tremendous start, turning profitable in just our third month. Businesswise we were fine, but the opportunity to get into the Columbia market had seemingly vanished. We were unhappy campers.

Enter Jim Weitzman, partner at the firm of Shrinsky, Weitzman and Eisen…and our FCC counsel. Like Mighty Mouse, Jim was there to save the day.

"No problem," sez Jim. "We'll file an application to change WSSL's City of License to someplace outside of the 'ninety mile limit' and we'll get the grant. But we have to be sure we work under the radar of the guy who turned us down. These government bureaucrats can be very vengeful, especially when they've been 'one-upped' (I say outfoxed)…which is what we'll be doing.

“So…find some place north of Laurens, a town, a settlement, a burg, even a crossroads. Make sure it has a Post Office and maybe a store or two…but no ‘radio service’, i.e. no radio station licensed to it.

Some background: The City of License (CL) concept dates back to the Communications Act of 1930, when many cities and towns had no local radio station existing for the sole purpose of ‘serving’ the people living in that city. I can assure you – fifty-two years later (1982) the industry had completely changed. There were more than enough radio stations.

Besides, all a radio station had to do to remain in compliance with FCC rules was provide one or two hours of ‘Meet The Mayor’ (or some other ginned-up local Public Affairs Programming) and broadcast it Sunday mornings between 7 and 9 AM. In other words, programming to which no one listened.

Re Plenty of Stations:

In 1980, The FCC mounted an attack on ‘the problem of too many stations’ by enacting Docket 80-90. This led to the creation of dozens more commercial FM stations, many of which joined the already large fraternity of financially failing radio stations.

Why did they fail?

Radio stations need revenue in order to pay salaries and other expenses. For that revenue radio stations depend heavily upon the sale of advertising, but the money available for radio advertising is finite and does not proportionally increase each time a new station goes on the air.

To that add the fact that all radio stations are not created equal. Small-footprint stations vs large footprint stations is a disaster for the small footprint stations. You get it, right?

“We’ll file an application to change the city of license from Laurens to your ‘burg of choice’. A few weeks after the grant we'll quietly re-file the application to move the WIGL tower. All will be well."

(Question: Is all of this machination simply insane or is it just me?)

Our 'Burg Of Choice' was Gray Court, SC - population then about 650. We filed the application to change our CL.

It was granted.

(What? No radio station can be heard in Gray Court? How about those thirty+ stations in Greenville, Spartanburg and Anderson? Puh-leeze.)

A few weeks later we reapplied for the Orangeburg tower relocation, which was also granted. WSSL was now a 'Gray Court' radio station.

All of this was done 100% within the existing rules.

Note: Later we heard that the guy who denied us the first time around was madder than a wet hen when he discovered what we'd done. Awwww.

So with all the tap dancing and paperwork out of the way it was time to hang the antenna and compete in Columbia, but there was a big problem. The Columbia market already had a very successful 100-kw Country station. Taking them on with WIGL would have been insane.

A few days after the antenna re-location (1985) we changed the call letters from WIGL to 'WTCB – B 1 0 6' and changed the format to HOT A C. The station has been successful in that format ever since.

Note: Gray Court, SC is the smallest City of License in America to which is licensed a full Class C 100-kw FM.

Performance

Radio broadcasting is all about people, the people who serve on the station staff. We hired Tom Love, gave him solid back office support and a boatload of ideas...and got out of his way. In 1982 WPJS produced annual revenue of $365,000.00. By 1984 WIGL's annual revenue was over $1,170,000.00.

A WSSL'n and WIGL'n Hiney

A crazy radio guy from Dayton, OH named Terry Dorsey created 'Hiney Wine', a mythical wine meant to serve as comedy material for his show. Along with hilarious fake 'commercials' he created lots of swag – t-shirts, ball caps, wine glasses, etc. It was an instant smash hit.

He put Hiney up for syndication. We bought the rights to Hiney Wine for WSSL and WIGL and promoted it like the dickens. Reaction was 'over the top'. Everybody was talking about it.

And trying to find the winery! Here's the scoop.

The 'winery' was owned and operated by the fictional Hiney Brothers, Big Red and Thor... *(Say it with me now: Big Red Hiney. Thor Hiney.).* Additional family members included (say it loud) sister Ophelia Hiney and Uncles Harry Hiney and Seymour Hiney.

As the promotional story went, the 'winery' was usually 'located' in a small town somewhere in the remote coverage area of the participating station.

On WSSL (Greenville, SC) we located the winery in Pelzer, SC. For WIGL (Columbia, SC) the winery was in Swansea, SC,"...behind the library."

On hearing the commercials, listeners began driving to Pelzer and Swansea in search of the 'winery'. Seriously.

Upon learning this was a hoax you'd think folks would be angry, and some were. Most thought it was great fun.

Not the Mayor and Town Lawyer of Swansea. Can you say ANGREE!

Actually they were madder'n hell!

About ten days after we started the promotion, these Swansea officials sent us an order to Cease and Desist.

Special Delivery!

"Too many people are disrupting the peace and quiet of the library by stopping to ask where the winery is located. Besides…it's a hoax. Get that damn thing off the air or we're gonna sue!"

Spoilsports, I say.

I wanted our lawyer to send them a letter recommending that they "…grab a Hiney and relax." Instead, we went on the air and announced that the winery had burned to the ground but "…let not your hearts be troubled. The Hiney Brothers – Big Red and Thor – will be re-opening in Horatio, SC."

Note: Before announcing the re-location Tom Love called the Mayor of Horatio to get his OK. "Hell yes," he said. "Bring it on."

Folks were laughing at the commercials and buying up fistfuls of the swag – golf shirts, t-shirts, ball caps, buttons, logoed wine glasses and Frisbees, et al.

"Hey there. We offer only the best. You can never have too much Hiney."

Or…

"Looking for a way to relax after dinner? Go ahead. Grab a Hiney."

But the best one of all was when the Hiney Brothers announced that Hiney Wine was now available in custom-made cans with an ice hole so folks could put ice or fruit in their Hiney.

Go ahead – say it. "Your Hiney now has an ice hole."

I double-dare you,

See what I mean!

There's so much more to tell about Hiney Wine and how big this syndication became. This was all our friends in Aiken could talk about…and the WIGL antenna was sixty miles to the east.

Following are some links where you'll find more laughs…at Hiney's expense.

Hiney Wine Fan C;lub
http://hineywinery.com/

Hiney Wine 'Commercial'
https://www.youtube.com/watch?v=MTUh_K28X7g

For Kerby and me the Hiney Wine campaign was every bit as crazy as anything we'd done when we were nutso Top Forty DJ's in the sixties. (See ALIAS EMPEROR RODGERS at emperorrodgers.com/)

Note: By 1979 our quest to develop great radio stations had settled into a programming formula that balanced three primary ingredients: News/Local Information (inclusive of professional-sounding commercials), Entertainment (inclusive of solid on-air personnel and lots of 'out of the studio – in the market' presence), and Demographically-aimed Music. 'Hiney Wine' fit perfectly in the 'Entertainment' section of this three-part concept, the part that read "Whenever it's appropriate - Keep it light. Keep it fun."

Hiney Wine Radio 'Ad'
https://www.youtube.com/watch?v=ZHgmr3DnJRg

One of my Aiken friends, a WIGL listener and Hiney Wine fan, created a 'toon for me.

OK, 'nuff said.

Now if you'll excuse me, I'm going to go get some Hiney.

CHAPTER 14
A REAL COMPANY

Early in 1983 we rented an office in Aiken.

Kerby Confer and Paul Rothfuss

The Williamsport, PA stations, WHUM (Reading, PA) and Cortland,NY stations had been sold. KSSN (Little Rock, AR), WSSL (Greenville, SC), WJDX-AM/WMSI-FM (Jackson, MS) and

WIGL (soon to be Columbia, SC) had been acquired, and we were getting bombarded with calls from brokers with stations for sale.

Note From our 'No Mystery Here' Department: In any industry, when it becomes a known fact that 'sufficient money' is backing a company, deals begin to flow toward that company. Deal-seekers don't want to waste time with anyone who can't close, and if you don't have the money...

Thanks to Jason Shrinsky we had in place a very serious business arrangement with TA Associates, and they were excited about what we were doing. With TA's financial wind filling our sails, our track record quickly revealed us to be people who made quick 'yes-no' decisions, and when the answer was 'yes' moved like lightning.

A call from TA would soon illustrate just how serious this had become.

Short version – Richard Churchill: "You guys are doing great and we're happy to be on board but we need you to hire a CFO post-haste. We want you to grow, but in order for us to continue doing business we need to be absolutely sure that you are in control of the financial side of your company, so we'll need frequent reporting.

You trying to provide that would be a waste of your time and talent. Get yourself a good CFO, like *yesterday*."

Kerby knew Donald Alt, the CFO of TM Productions. He recommended that we talk to Donald, who joined us shortly thereafter.

Note: We could not have found a better CFO if we'd looked for another year. Donald was the perfect fit at the perfect time. He's one of the smartest and savviest people I've ever known.

"And you also need a lawyer."

And we got a great one, Robert F. Wright, Jr., Esq. by name. Bob was a member of Augusta's leading law firm - Nixon, Yow, Waller and Capers, where he'd been concentrating his efforts on family trusts and estate planning.

I'm sure that representing a couple of mercurial Yankee ex-disc jockeys had never appeared on Bob's radar, but there we were. In short order Bob had his arms around what we were doing and it was 'off to the races'.

Bob is a no-nonsense guy, both 'understated' and brilliant. And he's a great negotiator. Sometimes the folks on 'the other side' tended to underestimate Bob. Many did.

At their own peril.

Advantage, us!

Note: I could tell you stories, but suffice it to say Bob steered us through deal negotiations and contracts with the skill of a rafting captain steering tourists through white-water rapids. He's a wonderful friend and a helluva hunting and fishing buddy. I miss those days.

Tusks Are Looser

Marx Brothers joke: "Why should we hunt elephants in Alabama?

"Because the tusks are looser." [Definitely a '9' on the Moan-Ometer!]

Jay Bowles called us with an opportunity. WTBC-AM and WUOA-FM in Tuscaloosa, Alabama were being offered for sale. WUOA-FM was a full Class C with the market's biggest footprint. The stations were the flagship for the Crimson Tide Sports Network.

Mr. Bert Bank

The stations were owned by Mr. Bert Bank, a former Alabama State Senator. Jay, Kerby and I flew to Tuscaloosa where we were met at the airport by Mr Bank.

The three of us got into Mr. Bank's Mercury Grand Marquis for the ride to the stations, Jay and Kerby in the back seat and me 'riding shotgun'. From this vantage point I had a close-up view of Mr. Bank as he adjusted his seat as far forward as it would go.

After starting the engine he leaned over the steering wheel as far as he could, as if to get his eyes closer to the windshield.

(So he could see better?)

Hesitatingly I asked, "Ahmmm, Mr. Bank…would you like me to drive"?

I was too late.

Leaning and squinting, he put the car in 'Drive' as he was saying, "No, no…I'm OK. It's just that my eyesight isn't what it used to be."

(Not exactly a confidence builder.)

In the back seat, Kerby and Jay shifted nervously as Mr. Bank eased out onto the Interstate – as if he'd been making this drive for years. He remained 'forwardly placed' at the wheel for the agonizingly short and thankfully safe trip to the station. I made a vow to rent a car for any future trips.

Note: Bert Bank was both the founder of the radio stations and of the University of Alabama Sports Network – and a personal friend of Paul 'Bear' Bryant, the legendary Alabama Football Coach. Mr. Bank was also a WWII War Hero, a survivor of the Bataan Death March which caused his eyesight to be compromised. He was captured in April of 1942 and held by the Japanese until being rescued by US Rangers in the Raid at Cabanatuan on January 30, 1945. Mr. Bank is the author of "Back From The Living Dead" a book recounting his time in captivity.

Pulling this deal together proved uneventful. George O'Rear was the GM and Susan Richards the GSM, two young people who made an excellent management team.

Performance

We changed the FM call letters to 'WFFX – The Fox'. We kept the staff intact, added the usual Kerby and Paul stuff (lots of ideas and promotions and 'out of station' activity) and watched as George and Susan took the revenue from $634,000 (1983) to $1, 081,000 (1985).

Miss Gertrude

A year or so after the closing, Kerby and I drove to Tuscaloosa to check out the stations and say hello to Mr. Bank. Our wives were with us, so Mr. Bank invited us to join he and his wife, Gertrude, for dinner at the beautiful North River Yacht Club.

'Miss Gertrude' was a lovely lady and it was a lovely evening.

Mr. Bank had been a State Senator for many years, so it was natural for the dinner conversation to turn toward politics. The ladies were mostly silent (actually, Miss Gertrude was completely so) as Mr. Bank, Kerby and I went on and on. "I'm for this"…"I couldn't support that"…"not so sure you're right" – etc., etc.

Back and forth we went and then, in one of those magic moments of silence that can suddenly appear in the midst of a conversation, Miss Gertrude spoke.

"Well," she said firmly, "I have only one thing to say."

"*I* am opposed to *anything* that restricts the mind."

The end!

Note #1: If you are a history buff you will want to read 'Back From The Living Dead'. No Hollywood soft soap here, this is a first-hand account of Mr. Banks' time in captivity. Mr.Bank passed away June 22, 2009. He was in his ninety-fifth year.

Note #2: I once asked Mr. Bank if he held a grudge against the Japanese. He said, "No not at all. I've no time for such things. Too much to do."

Note #3: If you find yourself in Tuscaloosa with a yearning for great BBQ, be sure to visit Dreamland.

'Nother'un

Bowles was back, this time with an AM/FM combo licensed to Russellville, Kentucky, population 6,000. WRUS-AM, a 1 kw daytimer at 610 on the dial, and WAKQ-FM, licensed to broadcast with 100kw @ 2,000' HAAT.

Sidebar: Russellville was famous for being home to the world's largest One-Sucker Tobacco auction. One Sucker Tobacco is an all-purpose, dark, air-cured tobacco that was used for snuff, chewing, cigarettes and cigar blending. One Sucker produces fewer suckers (flowering stalks), a desirable trait for tobacco-leaf growers.

WRUS was a very successful local station, mainly because their morning man, Don Neagle, had been there for years and was a mainstay in the community.

WAKQ-FM, 'KQ-101', was in a rock format.

A new tall tower was constructed and the FM antenna hung @ 1,300' HAAT throwing a 60-dbu signal over Bowling Green to the east, and Hopkinsville, KY and Clarksville, TN to the west. We guessed they'd chosen the Rock format in order to reach the college students at Western Kentucky University in Bowling Green and the military folks at Fort Campbell in Clarksville. We noted that, with the exception of the Nashville stations some seventy miles to the south, the region had no Country music FM station.

For Kerby and me, *this* was the opportunity.

We bought the stations and got busy preparing for a format change and the mandatory re-imaging.

Call Letter 'Never Do's

In researching call letters one always encounters certain sets of calls that will never be used. You can imagine what they'd be.

For example, if WNNK can be interpreted and promoted as 'WINK' and WSSL can be 'WHISTLE', it's easy to understand why no radio station would ever use WPIS (sorry). You get the picture.

For most broadcasters 'WBVR' was also a 'Never Do'. This *had* to be the case, otherwise it would have been taken.

WBVR was tops on my list.

Mind Over Assumption

My bet? Probably due to the Merle Haggard/Leona Williams hit Country song, 'The Bull And The Beaver', broadcasters envisioned listeners drawing a negative connotation from these call letters, thus causing a negative reaction to any radio station that might choose WBVR.

I believed 'WBVR – The Beaver' was perfect for a Country station, and that a well-planned and orchestrated 'image pre-sell' would easily offset most objections.

It took a teeny bit of convincing but I finally convinced Kerby (this didn't take *too* much doing) and we went for it.

The Plan

A week or so before the format change we inundated the area with a billboard campaign that I believed would cement 'the proper image' for the station.

At the same time, we distributed cute little stuffed-animal beavers wearing yellow t-shirts with the station call letters prominently displayed.

Clients got 'em. So did listeners.

We changed formats and let 'er rip.

There was a protest call or two. Otherwise, we pulled it off without a hitch.

Performance

The format change from Rock to Country was accompanied by a change of call letters (from WAKQ to WBVR) and a complete re-imaging. We added new management and sales people to the staff, along with what by now had become our standard operating formula.

In 1983, revenue for WAKQ/WRUS (Jan. to July) and WBVR/WRUS (July to Dec.) was $731,000. In our first full calendar year (1985) WBVR/WRUS revenue exceeded $1,050,000.

Note: Over the years I've had the good fortune to meet many outstanding broadcast professionals. Don Neagle is among the finest of these. Talented. Dedicated. Loyal. Aware. Community involved. Decades of excellence at the same radio station. For all of these 'right reasons' Don deserves a plaque in the National Broadcast Hall Of Fame.

Moving Day

The acquisition of all these properties (plus what was on the horizon) quickly led to the creation of a multi-staff accounting department headed by Donald Alt, meaning that we needed more office space.

We moved into Rosemary Hall, a beautiful old home on Carolina Avenue in North Augusta, SC that had been converted into elegant office space.

Today Rosemary Hall is Rosemary Inn, a top-of-the-line Bed and Breakfast. Go online and google "The History of Rosemary Hall" Quite extraordinary.

Nearby Opportunity

For quite some time Kerby and I had been aware of an AM/FM combo in Augusta that was badly in need of help (I believe the call letters were WAUG AM/FM. Not sure.)

The AM was a 'throw-away daytimer' @ 1050. The FM was a full Class C, licensed to broadcast with 100-kw @ 2000' HAAT but tragically undeveloped...technically, formatically, and businesswise.

In other words - opportunity!

The stations were located on low-lying ground along the Savannah River, south of the city on Sand Bar Ferry Road. The FM antenna hung on the 200 foot AM tower.

Short version: There could not have been a worse location for this FM.

Just across the river on the South Carolina side stood the tall tower of a local TV station, a short two miles from the FM antenna location. Some elementary digging revealed that a minor change application would permit the FM antenna to be relocated to that tower.

I don't remember the name of the person who owned the station. He knew he 'had something' but he didn't have the moxie to 'lay it all on the line' and go for it. Or perhaps he didn't know how.

It took us several months of pleading and cajoling but finally he agreed to sell us the stations, after which we negotiated a long-term deal with (I believe) Channel Six to hang the antenna on their tower @ 1,217 ' HAAT.

Early in 1984 we closed the deal and dropped our application to change the antenna location.

Market Overview

There was one other full Class C FM in the market. Legendary WBBQ was the way-ahead market leader, doing Top Forty with a 28-share of the audience. Simply a 'killer' radio station in every way.

Among the 'also-rans' was WGUS, a Class A FM (3-kw @ 300' HAAT) with a 13-share doing Country.

We saw no advantage in going head-to-head with WBBQ, but because their audience was heavily skewed toward listeners 12 – 34 we decided to go with a Hot AC format aimed at women 25 – 54. We played all the current hits that were not hard rock, plus a liberal inclusion of the great Oldies from 1958 thru the seventies.

We changed the call letters to 'WZNY – SUNNY 105'. By early summer we hung the antenna, turning this flickering match-head of a radio signal into a giant flame-thrower, quintupling the station footprint.

SUNNY was an instant hit with our target demographic. I knew this because we lived in Aiken, SC, part of the Augusta metro. All of our female Aiken friends were in our desired demographic. They knew we owned the station and were 'all over me' telling me how much they loved it.

Early station ratings confirmed our success. WBBQ remained the overall #1 station, but SUNNY was #1 with females, 25 – 54, the 'money' demographic.

For our station mascot, we had our graphic artist draw us a picture of the sun as if it were a cute little guy, alive and on foot. We took his drawing to our 'costume maker' and PRESTO! Sunny Ray was born. Children loved him. Adults too!

Performance

The awakening of this giant FM was amazing. In a flash the station footprint went from mouse-like to elephantine. We built a staff from scratch - top to bottom. We opened the promotional floodgates and gave the station an easy-to-remember name and image. And we got out into the community.

Other than 'peanuts', I can't remember exactly what station revenue was when we bought it. By 1986 the annual revenue at SUNNY 105 was in excess of $1,000,000.00 en route to over $2-million.

You Can't Make This Up

In 'ALIAS EMPEROR RODGERS' I described how Kerby and I began our radio careers at WMPT in South Williamsport, PA, a new radio station that was put on the air in 1957 by Galen D. 'Dave' Castlebury shortly after he mustered out of the army from Fort Gordon...in (ulp!) Augusta, GA.

While being stationed at Ft. Gordon, Dave was also employed part time by WAUG AM/FM where at 'muster time' he had accumulated lots and lots of hours yet unpaid. On the night he departed Augusta for Pennsylvania, Dave helped himself to some unused equipment as 'payment for back wages owed', including a five-pot GE FM board which he installed at WMPT.

This was the very board that Kerby and I used at our first radio job.

How strange is that? (Insert 'Twilight Zone' theme music here.)

A Golf-related Aside

The Masters Golf Tournament is played in Augusta each April. Local radio stations are asked to help by broadcasting local information for the thousands of fans who come to town, in return for which the stations are given badges to attend the tournament.

Neither Donald nor Kerby cared that much for golf but I loved the game. For the next several years I 'confiscated' some of the badges and attended the tournament. It was fabulous.

In 1986 I was on the spectator mound between the seventeenth green and the fifteenth fairway when Jack Nicklaus made his birdie putt en route to victory, the film of which I bet you've seen. Nicklaus' raised putter was pointed directly at where I was standing.

The very next year I was sitting along the ropes near the eleventh green when Larry Mize chipped it in to beat Greg Norman.

'Tis the truth, I swear.

The AIMS Group

At about this time we were invited to join AIMS – the Association of Independent Metropolitan Stations. AIMS was started in the early 1950's when television usurped the network shows that had been the staple of radio programming for so long. (Before this time, radio's place in the entertainment culture was 'TV without pictures'.) Because 'two heads are better than one' a group of now-independent broadcasters decided to get together to discuss what they needed to do in order to stay in business.

The group was limited to ten members, all of whom either owned or were the CEO of groups of radio stations. Guests were permitted to attend meetings but there could be but one 'member' per group. Kerby was our representative.

AIMS met three times per year to share information about everything from sales and promotional ideas to the handling of employee problems, listener complaints, and FCC problems. Businesswise, no subject was too sensitive to be brought up for discussion. Everything was 'on the table'. Attendance was mandatory – no excuses. The penalty for non-attendance was expulsion.

Recall our emphasis on 'ideas'. AIMS was the ultimate idea source...on steroids. Re Sales and Promotion, members would bring complete information to each meeting about everything their stations had done in the previous quarter, all neatly assembled in notebooks, one book for each member.

Each member was given one hour to stand before the group and go through their information, explaining details and answering questions. Each item included every minute detail of the promotion or the sales idea. That way the other members could go back to their stations and seamlessly use it on their station if they chose.

The Chairman of AIMS was Dick Chapin, at that time the COO of Stuart Broadcasting based in Lincoln, NE, one of the finest broadcasters and finest people I ever met...and a legend. At this writing Mr. Chapin is ninety-six.

Many other great broadcasters were AIMS members when we joined. Joe Amaturo, Mel Cooper, Myron Jones, Stan Kaplan, Paul Palmer and Jim Tazarek to name a few. Great men all, and very helpful to us and our company.

Now You Got It...

So Jay Bowles is on the phone again.

This time he had listed a full Class C FM licensed to Hammond, Louisiana, with a construction permit to build a 1000-foot tower some thirty miles to the west, hang the antenna and put a dynamite signal over Baton Rouge. Our research revealed that Baton Rouge had but five viable radio stations, four FM and one AM. Perfect!

We were off to Hammond, the Duck Hunting Capital of the World.

The station was owned by Ron Strother and Donald Lobell. Strother was the broadcaster. Lobell was the 'investor'...and also an egg farmer. If memory serves he had a huge flock of laying hens and was selling eggs all over Louisiana.

(Lobell was also an outstanding joke-teller – one of the best ever. I remember one story that ended with the punch line 'Sheep lie'. I laughed for days.)

We met with these two gentlemen on a Tuesday. They were asking $1.7 million for the station. By four that afternoon we'd agreed on the purchase price and promised to have contracts in their hands by the following Monday. We shook hands on the deal and were off to the airport.

Pertinent information was given to Bob Wright and sure enough, Friday afternoon Bob had our signed contracts ready for Federal Express delivery to the Seller the following Monday (copies to Jay Bowles).

...Now You Don't!

Monday morning we anxiously awaited the good news from Bowles. "The contract has been signed. Go ahead and post the escrow."

Jay called around 11:30 with a much different message.

"They sold it to someone else."

Jay continued: "On Friday these guys flew their private plane to Hammond, picked up Ron Strother and took him to New Orleans for a weekend of wine, women and song.

(I've always questioned the 'song' part...if you catch my drift.)

"Strother was so 'impressed' he signed a Letter of Intent on the spot. Sorry guys."

Oh well...

CHAPTER 15
THE BIG TRIP

Kerby returned from the January AIMS meeting with an idea that, if implemented properly, had the potential to seriously increase our revenue. As always with the ideas shared by the AIMS members, this one came complete with instructions.

First, contact a really good travel agent and ask them to formulate a list of outstanding European trips costing no more than $3,500.00 for two people ($8,500.00 today), the trips to include airfare, the best hotels and restaurants and lots of great 'stuff' for folks to see and do.

Next, from that list select a trip and offer it as a premium to prospects (*new business*) who agree to spend $25,000.00 with your station in the next twelve months, *or* to current clients who agree to increase their spending by, say, $15,000.00.

(*"You'll want to get with your General Managers and Sales Managers to carefully select the businesses you want to approach with this. You should also consider offering this to existing clients who've been spending over $20,000.00 with you for at least the past two years."*)

Last, if you do this, *be sure to make the final night of the trip memorable.*

We agonized about this. If our stations were in top-fifty markets with high-dollar rate cards it would have been a no-brainer. Most of our stations were top-rated and usually commanded the highest ad rates in their markets, but they were all in medium-sized markets.

Using our 'Fire, Ready, Aim' method, we decided to go for it.

Herr Karl Wolfgang Helft

For our travel agent we chose Karl Helft, a naturalized American citizen who grew up in Germany where his father owned a mill. At age fifteen (late 1944) Karl was conscripted into the Hitler Youth and sent to work at a munitions dump in the northern part of Germany.

Note: Karl returned home after the Germans surrendered [May, 1945]. A short time later his father learned that the area in which they resided was to be a part of East Germany and thus would be controlled by the Russians. Upon learning this Herr Helft gave ownership of the mill to his foreman, gathered Karl and the rest of his family and fled to the west, with Karl eventually arriving in America.

The unforgettable, ebullient, Karl W. Helft

In addition to being a top-notch travel agent (he knew Europe like the back of his hand) Karl was a student of the European railroad system, the #1 mode of mass transportation in that part of the world. This unique combination of knowledge enabled Karl to pull together European trips that were wonderful beyond imagination.

Switzerland

Our first Big Trip was to Lucerne and Interlachen, Switzerland. About one-hundred people joined us on this trip - eighty-five clients and significant others plus fifteen of our radio colleagues. And of course, Karl Helft, our official Tour Guide and 'Euro Expert'. Our clients peppered Karl with questions, questions, questions, which he answered enthusiastically.

(By trip's end many were asking Karl to be their travel agent.)

We enjoyed a bus trip to the Matterhorn (it's a *really tall Alp @14,692 feet above sea-level, a great spot for an FM antenna. LOL)* and to Gruyere (fabulous little town...great cheese, too!).

And shopping. Oh my, the shopping!

Whilst in Switzerland I got a 'music lesson' on the alpenhorn...

Alpenhorn figurine.

Best of all was three nights in Interlaken at the luxurious Victoria Jungfrau Hotel. And of course, the shopping.

One of the evenings there featured an evening boat ride across a lake to the opulent Casino Lucarno - men in tux and ladies in evening dress. I'd never been to Las Vegas and am not a casino gambler, but I adore new experiences and 'evenings out' with my bride. Barbie and I had an absolute ball watching folks root for 'three-plums-in-a-row' on the slot machines or shouting exhortations at the Shooter as he rolled out the dice at the Craps table.

I don't know how to say, "C'mon with a Skinny Dugan" in Italian, but I'm sure folks were both rooting for and against ol' Skinny, as the dice tumbled their way to pairings that favored some and really po'ed others. No matter. They all came back for more. Win, lose, or draw ... most of the clients who chose this excursion said they absolutely loved it.

(BTW - In Craps parlance a 'Skinny Dugan' is a seven.)

Makin' Memories

For the last night of our Big Trip, Karl arranged for an elegant dinner party in the main dining room of the Victoria Jungfrau...the entire group in attendance, men in tuxedos and ladies in evening dress.

Generous cocktails preceded a five-course dinner, then a fabulous selection of cheeses and fruits. Dessert? Glad you asked. Baked Alaska if you please.

And revelry throughout.

Simply stated, this was a fabulous evening. Our clients told us so.

Paul & Barbie, out to dinner in Switzerland.

What's this? A Barbershop Quartet? In Switzerland? Nah. Just 'the suits'.

(l-r) The Partners - Kerby Confer, Donald Alt, Jerry Atchley, Paul Rothfuss

(Ya know what? We were a lot younger then!)

Throughout the trip our clients were effusive in their praise. "Great food." "Beautiful Hotel." "Loved the casino." "So much to see and do." "The Matterhorn. Wow"! "Great food."

And perhaps best of all, "Where are we going next year"?

The Take-Away

We calculated total ad sales of $900,000.00 across all markets, at least 70% of which was new business. Our total cost, radio folks included, was about $170,000.00. Our first Big Trip was a big success, as were those that followed.

For 1985, Karl planned our Big Trip for ...

Munich and Vienna

Germany's Bernhard Langer won the Masters Golf Tournament in April and I was curious about the relative popularity of golf in West Germany.

While checking into our hotel in Munich I asked the young lady at the desk if she knew of Bernhard Langer. She shook her head 'no'. I explained why I was asking, then inquired as to how in German I would ask others if they knew about him.

She replied, "Just say "Kennen sie ('do you know'), then say his name."

There was a band playing oom-pah music when we registered. I noticed they were taking a break so I took the opportunity to approach the bandleader.

After saying our hellos I asked him, "Kennen sie Bernhard Langer"?

Bandleader (quizzically, shaking his head): "Bernhard Langer? Mmmm, nein."

Me (taking a shot with my German): "Der golfspieler."

Bandleader (shaking his head): "Ahh...golfspieler.

"Golf? In Deutchland?

"Nicht!"

Fame is fickle.

Barbie The Linguist

One of our station managers, Mike Steinhilper, was a host for this Big Trip. We were standing in the lobby with Mike, who seemed fixated on the prospect of drinking some German beer. At one point Mike told us that he didn't know German, which he thought would be a problem.

Barbie piped up with, "Oh Mike, don't worry about that. All you have to do is say 'en sie' at the end of your sentences. If you want someone to come over to you just say, "Come en sie", or if you want them to sit down just say "Sit en sie". It works great."

"Really?" said Mike.

"Yes...really."

And Mike was outta there, in a quest to find German beer.

(Barbie didn't know German, but whattheheck.)

A little while later we, too, were off to find Hofbräuhaus München where we hoped to get a beer. On arrival we saw our boy Mike, enjoying a stein o' beer and 'conversation' with one of the local fellows.

Excitedly, Mike waved at us and said, "OmiGod, Barbie. You won't believe this. I was only here for a few minutes when Hans here came walking by, lookin' for a place to sit. I pointed at the bench across from me and said, "Sit en sie"...and the guy sat down! It really worked."

It must have been the beer talking.

Merriment on the Orient Express

'Twas time to head for Vienna.

Karl arranged for us to make the trip in two railroad cars from the Orient Express, a club car and a dining car complete with two cute frauleins to wait on us, and a liveried butler who also served as a bartender.

The train left promptly at 8:45 AM en route to Salzburg. By nine we were being served a wonderful brunch complete with generous glasses of German white wine.

Our noontime stop in Salzburg featured lunch and a bit of sightseeing, then back on the train for the ride to Vienna. More German white wine (hic!) and Q&A with Herr Helft.

Mid-afternoon in Vienna found us with an hour or two for sightseeing, then a late afternoon mini-concert that Karl had arranged exclusively for our group.

The Vienna Boys Choir is a world-famous group of musically talented boy sopranos, most of whom are under age thirteen (no baritones or basses please). Describing their sound is impossible. Crystal-clear for starters. Magical. Innocent. Perfect. And in many ways, Angelic.

Our group was enthralled.

The Finale

Off to the hotel to freshen and change for dinner.

Around 7 PM Karl guided us to a for-realsie castle for cocktails and another five-course gourmet dinner, et cetera. (It would be easy to get used to this!)

A string octet played beautiful music during dinner and then long into the evening.

The German wine flowed freely.

Barbie and I waltzed the night away.

Our group was most impressed.

Note: Karl Helft was a living encyclopedia – the difference-maker for our trips. Herr Helft passed away in November, 2017. He was eighty-eight. "Gute Arbeit mein Freund."

North To Alaska

In 1986, again with a passel of clients and significant others, we boarded a Norwegian Cruise Line ship for an eight day cruise to Alaska, and the many day trips that came with it.

(l-r) Judy Confer, Kerby Confer, Paul Rothfuss, Barbie Rothfuss

The ship sailed into Glacier Bay for a close-up view of the calving of the glaciers, then on to Ketchikan where some of us fished for salmon.

We were allowed to keep a maximum of two fish each, with each fish weighing a minimum of ten pounds. I was fortunate to catch two of these beauties. I took the fish back to the ship where they were properly wrapped and quick-frozen.

At trips end, the fish were given to us as we left the ship. I further wrapped my fish in some clothing and put 'em in a suitcase. The day after we arrived home I smoked and refrigerated fifteen pounds of fresh salmon which we enjoyed (one delicious piece at a time) for the remainder of 1986. Yum!

One of the day trips found us in a small open boat with twenty-five people, watching in awe from thirty yards away as a pod of humpback whales formed bubble nets. One whale, mouth agape, emerged from the center of the 'net' having feasted on the krill that was 'trapped' inside.

The next stop was Juneau for shopping (of course), and a day trip to Skagway with a visit to the Klondike Gold Rush National Historical Park. Fascinating history there. Those were tough times.

Note: "North To Alaska" - Johnny Horton's hit record of 1960 - is the story of the Alaskan Gold rush. The song reached #4 on the Billboard Top 100 chart. Skagway was the 'jumping off place' for the miners.

And of course we shopped!

Alaskan gift shops were unique in that many featured items crafted by native Alaskans, Inuit et al. Many of the shops offered outstanding examples of scrimshaw – artwork etched on ivory.

Speaking of Scrimshaw

The harvesting and/or importing of 'new' ivory has been illegal since 1989, however scrimshanders are permitted to practice the art of scrimshaw if the ivory used was obtained before 1989, or if they are Native American.

Check this out.

This is an ancient whales tooth on which the artist has rendered an act seen on the African veldt nearly every day - a cheetah in pursuit of a Thompson's gazelle. It was purchased in Ketchikan. Sadly it is unsigned.

The Personal Touch

Perhaps our biggest dividend was the opportunity for our ownership and station management group to spend personal time with some of our best, and in many cases our newest, clients. We got to know each other in a totally relaxed, non-business atmosphere - all fun, all the time. A great way to do business without doing business.

I don't recall even one complaint that I would describe as 'major' coming from any of the folks who joined us on any of the trips.

Our trips were Five Star all the way. Our clients loved them.

I'd do it again in a heartbeat.

(If you haven't seen Alaska, this is a great way to go. Contact Norwegian Cruise Lines today!

D-Day, And The Red Sticky

What follows may at first seem a bit 'off topic'. Thank you for your perseverance.

The whole of World War II took place when I was very young. On D-Day (June 6, 1944) I was three years old and the war itself had ended before my fifth birthday, so my impressions of the war are vague at best. I do recall Dad and Mom listening intently to newscasts on the radio, after which they'd talk about what they'd just heard. They always spoke in serious tones but really, at my age, I didn't understand much of what was going on.

Since that time, with thanks to excellent history teachers who piqued my interest, I've read lots of books and novels, watched many documentary films on The History Channel and Smithsonian, and learned a lot about WWII.

I was well aware of how badly England had been punished by the German military and how close they had come to defeat, but all the reading and documentary watching in the world could never have prepared me for the revelation I experienced some forty years after the war's end.

The Story

Our 'Big Trip' idea provided us with a really great perk.

So...you wouldn't send large groups of your best clients to places you'd never seen, right? What if the hotels and restaurants turned out to be dumps? The tax laws of the day allowed us to go abroad to 'vet' various places that we (someday) might want to send our clients...and write off the trips as business expenses.

(*Whoa there. Calm down. We didn't write these laws.)*

We were considering Great Britain as the destination for the next Big Trip, so June of 1985 found Barbie and me vacationing in England with Donald and Judy Alt and Kerby and Judy Confer - business partners and personal friends. All of us were in our early forties.

Oh, except for Judy C. She was younger. Much younger.

A ten-day trip was planned. We flew to London, rented a van, 'loaded up' and headed out, stopping to check out several small private hotels along the way. Several days into this 'laugh fest' we found ourselves in the city of Bath for a two-night stay, where our plans were about to change.

In the lobby of the hotel was a rack containing promotional brochures describing nearby sights and events that might be of interest to tourists. In perusing the selection Donald landed on a gem.

"Hey. Here's something we need to look into. A very old private residence called Cliveden (Cliv'- dn) is having their Grand Opening this weekend. It looks like a really special place. I think we should see if they have rooms available."

"Yes," replied the chorus.

Donald made the call and - Volia! – three rooms were available.

We grabbed 'em and started our three-hour drive east.

Ahhh Cliveden

The street..., er, driveway...ahmm, the road...ehh, no – 'The 'Entrance' to Cliveden was something out of a travelogue.

A long, winding lane guarded by big beautiful hardwood trees led us into a lovely courtyard, in the back of which was one of the most beautiful structures I'd ever seen.

'Twas Cliveden House, located on Cliveden Rd., Taplow, Maidenhead, UK.

(Google it and see for yourself.)

Cliveden House

We drove the van up to the portico where we were greeted by a Bellman and the Hotel Manager, as well as a few other people we assumed to be guests, one of whom was a well-dressed lady in her sixties.

The lady watched with interest as the bellman unloaded our van. Apparently amazed by the sheer amount of our luggage she said (rather loudly), "Is that all *your* luggage"?

In his most earnest tone Kerby replied, "Oh, no Ma'am. Our luggage lorry is expected to arrive shortly."

With that our new lady friend gasped, and then - fanning her face with her right hand, turned to go inside. Thankfully we were able to stifle our laughter thus avoiding the embarrassment that would surely have followed.

(Once a Disc Jockey, always a Disc Jockey!)

The manager showed us inside where we completed our registration and made off to our rooms.

Which were *gorgeous.*

Just outside our room was a veranda overlooking the beautiful gardens of Cliveden, and from which we could see the River Thames in the distance, winding its way through the English countryside. I remember thinking *'I bet heaven looks something like this'.*

Lord and Lady Orkney

Propped up on the pillows was an envelope containing an invitation to join the Manager and Guests for cocktails. "Five-Thirty, in the Great Room."

Promptly at five-thirty we joined the Manager and more than twenty guests for cocktails. We weren't in the room five minutes before our new lady friend came over and introduced herself.

"Welcome to Cliveden," she said. "I'm Lady Orkney and (pointing to an older gentleman sitting in a wing chair across the room) *that* is my husband, Lord Orkney. And you are from America."

"So tell me...is it true you all live like *Dinna'-stee*"? A reference to 'Dynasty', the TV show starring John Forsythe.

We laughed and assured her that this was not the case.

Every so often, as our pleasant small talk continued, Lady Orkney would look over to Lord Orkney who sat virtually expressionless and seemingly riveted to his chair. This appeared to be upsetting to Lady Orkney who suddenly volunteered, "You'll have to pardon Cecil. He's so...*eccentric."*

(I felt sorry for the poor fellow. He hadn't said a word.)

The Maître'd announced dinner and we went to our round table-for-six. Barbie was sitting on my right.

Dinner You Say? More Like A Feast.

We enjoyed a delicious English dinner: standing rib roast of beef (rare to medium rare), Yorkshire pudding, escalloped potatoes and a crisp salad of fresh vegetables, no doubt from the gardens of Cliveden. Next was a wonderful selection of cheeses followed by a generous slice of deep-dish apple pie à la mode. The coup de grâce was a yummy piece of chocolate.

As dessert was being served at our table I felt a hand on my right shoulder. I was surprised to find Lord Orkney standing between Barbie and me with Lady Orkney slightly behind him to his right.

"Pardon me Gentlemen," he said. "I don't mean to interrupt your dessert but I wonder: Would you care to join us for a red sticky"?

(I'm dead certain that not one of us would have known a 'red sticky' if it flopped down on the table in front of us. I know I didn't.)

Donald and Kerby thanked Lord Orkney and politely declined.

Barbie nodded immediately. "We'd be delighted," she said.

"Wonderful," he exclaimed. "Enjoy your dessert, then come to the Great Room. We'll have everything ready."

Unforgettable

Lord Orkney had chosen a cozy corner in the Great Room. There, a love seat faced two chairs with a coffee table in between. On the coffee table sat a bottle of what appeared to be red wine...and four small glasses.

Lord and Lady Orkney were each sitting in one of the chairs. As Barbie and I approached the love seat, Lord Orkney rose to shake my hand…and kiss Barbie's. "Welcome," he said. "I am Lord Orkney and this is Lady Orkney." I introduced the two of us and Lord Orkney motioned us to sit.

"May I pour you a red sticky"?

"Yes Sir, please do."

Lord Orkney lifted the bottle from the table and poured some red wine into the small glasses, which appeared to be specifically designed for this purpose.

Note: I was soon to learn that a 'Red Sticky' is a glass of Port Wine (red), so called because after one raises the glass to take a taste, the wine appears to 'stick' to the side of the glass as it recedes. It's a beautiful thing.

Lord Orkney raised his glass in a toast. "To friendship," he said.

We replied in kind.

Then Lord Orkney said, "I want to take this opportunity to say 'Thank You, Thank You, Thank You' for everything you Americans did for us those many years ago. You selflessly plunged into the Great War, committing men and armaments in ways never before seen in this world. On D-Day thousands of your boys, with little or no personal connection to any Englishman, dove without hesitation into the fray. Thousands gave their lives for us, a debt that can never be repaid. But you never demanded even a penny of repayment… or even suggested such a thing.

"No words can ever express our gratitude to you and to America. Again…Thank
You, Thank You, Thank You."

I was completely taken aback. Speechless, and with no idea at all about how to respond.

"Well...ahm...Sir...ahmm, you must know that I had nothing whatsoever to do with this. I was only four years old when the war ended and..."

Lord Orkney waved his hand, stopping me in mid-sentence.

"It matters not a whit. England is today and forever will be grateful to America. If not for America there would *be* no England. Please. You *must* understand that."

"Yes, Sir. Thank you Sir."

Amazing stuff, right?

The Invitation

As our time together was winding down Lord Orkney said, "This has been delightful and we want to see you again. Please...I want you to come to London and stay as my guest at a hotel near the House of Lords. We'll spend the week together...show you the sights. It will be wonderful."

We agreed that such a visit would indeed be delightful and thanked him for his generous invitation.

As we stood to leave, Lord Orkney picked up a wrapped package and handed it to Barbie. "With our compliments," he said. "Do enjoy the rest of your holiday."

Back in our room we carefully unwrapped the package.

Inside was a box of chocolates. Pressed into the top of each individual chocolate was the emblem of the House of Lords.

We hid the box in our luggage, 'saving it for later'. When we got home we put the chocolates in the fridge, after which 'from time to time' we enjoyed one, and reveled in the memory of Lord and Lady Orkney.

Sneaky us!

Our meeting with Lord and Lady Orkney was my first time to taste Port Wine, so named because it comes from Portugal. Port is now my favorite libation. Today, when I have a glass of Port I raise a toast to Lord Orkney and to that fine 'fellow' to whom he introduced us in 1985 - *Senhor Pegajoso Vermelho* ('Red Sticky' in Portuguese).

One of my very few regrets is that I was 'too busy' to stay in touch with Lord and Lady Orkney and to return to London as they requested. I had the freedom to do so but things like that slipped from my mind always to be replaced with thoughts of my family and building Keymarket Communications.

Recently I went to Wikipedia to learn more about Lord Orkney. I discovered that this fine gentleman had no children. Might that have been part of his reason for inviting us to return?

Cecil O'Bryen Fitz-Maurice, 8th Earl of Orkney
(3 July 1919 – 5 February 1998)
•news clip and succession chart from: http://fitzmaurice-family.com/orkney.html

AUG 25, 1951

NEW

Ancient Title For Buck Private

Cecil Fitz-Maurice, the new Earl of Orkney, gives the "thumbs-up" sign as he sits in the cab of his British Army lorry on the Korean western front where he is serving as a private. Fitz-Maurice, at age 21, became the eighth Earl of Orkney when a distant relative, the 84-year-old Earl of Orkney, died recently. He inherits money and a castle at Buckinghamshire. (AP)

The following historical information from:

https://en.wikipedia.org/wiki/Cecil_FitzMaurice,_8th_Earl_of_Orkney

Lord Orkney was a Scottish peer who held the subsidiary titles of Viscount of Kirkwall and Baron of Dechmont.

He was the younger son of Captain Douglas Frederick Harold FitzMaurice RNAS. His elder brother Douglas Hubert Hamilton FitzMaurice died in 1942, killed in action during the Second World War.

Lord Orkney joined the Royal Army Service Corps on the outbreak of the Second World War in 1939 and served in North Africa, Italy, France and Germany. He later served in the Korean War from 1950 to 1951. In 1951, he inherited the Earldom of Orkney from a cousin, Edmond Walter FitzMaurice, 7th Earl of Orkney.

In 1953, the new Lord Orkney married Rose Katharine Durk, the younger daughter of J. W. D. Silley, of Brixham. It was she who asked us about 'Dinna-stee'. They had no children.

Lord Orkney died in 1998 and was succeeded by his kinsman Oliver Peter St John.

With the granting of seats in the House of Lords to all Scottish peers, which took effect in August 1963, Orkney gained a seat in the Lords, which was then expected to be for life. He did not live to see the enactment of theHouse of Lords Act of 1999, which removed most hereditary peers and would have cost him his seat.

1st Earl of Shelburne to 8th Earl of Orkney

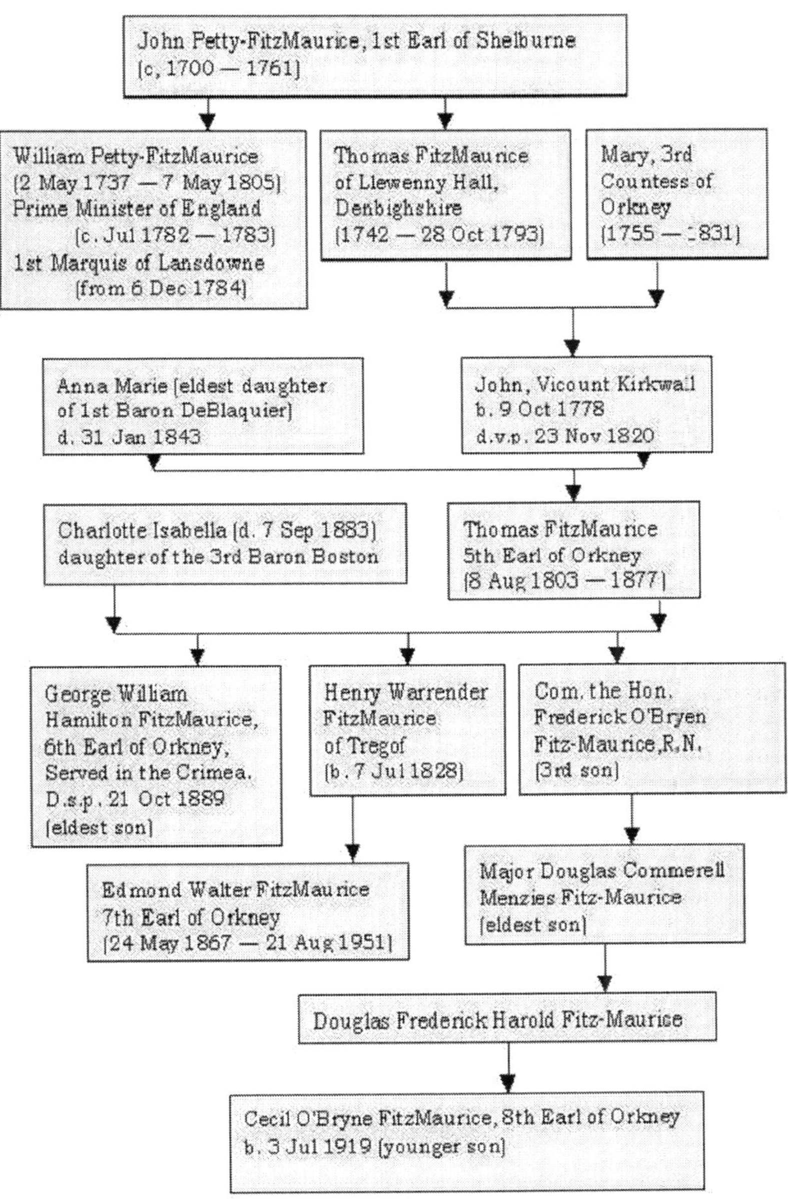

Succession Chart from:
http://fitzmaurice-family.com/orkney.html

CHAPTER 16
1984

Mid-1984 found us in acquisition frenzy, culminating in three closings in November.

First up, a most unexpected call from Jay Bowles.

Our receptionist: "Paul, Jay Bowles is on line two."

Me: "Jay, what's up"?

Jay: "It's baaaack."

Me: "What"?

Jay: "Baton Rouge. It's baaaack."

(You won't believe this story.)

"So…the guy who bought the station now wants to sell it. He figured y'all would be interested. He bought the station for $1.7 million. He's asking $2.7 million."

(Well kiss my sneakers and call me Keds. Ain't that just the derndest thing.)

Me: "What? Is this guy nuts? I could've had it for $1.7 million last year. Why would I pay $2.7 million for it nine months later"?

Jay: "Excuse me Paul but you're wrong. First, you *couldn't* have had it last year. If you *could* have had it you'd *have* it. But you don't.

"Next (*you're gonna love this little twist*) he'll take the extra million in a ten-year note, interest only for two years with a balloon at the end of six years. He refers to the note as his retirement plan. Given the time value of money and the way you guys turn stations around this one seems easy to me."

I was skeptical.

To my surprise, after Donald put pencil to paper he agreed with Jay.

We made the deal.

WKJN – 'KAJUN 103'

Recall that the FCC had approved a construction permit to relocate the antenna several miles to the west, enabling the station to throw a 60db signal over the entire Baton Rouge metro.

Our plan was to go head-to-head with an established Country FM that had been alone in the format for quite some time, sitting atop the Baton Rouge ratings with an eighteen share.

So, why a head-to-head battle?

To us, the established station sounded tired and unexciting...like they were 'taking it for granted'. Plus they were loaded with commercials — 25 minutes per hour loaded.

We believed if we hit 'em with our patented cool easy-to-remember call letters supported by dynamite 'connected' visuals, up-tempo jingles and personalities, our always-exciting promotions and our 'Three-In-A Row' formula - and if we got the station out of the studio and into the community - we'd grab a bunch of their listeners and advertisers.

And a bunch of their advertisers, too!

We hired Barry Drake to be our GM (PD at WLYC, our first; and 'stole' Mike Baer (a Louisiana native) from TM Productions to be our Sales Manager. One helluva team.

Next we scouted and hired a DJ who had previously been a top-rated morning host in the market, got a couple of other hot-shot personalities, bought a bunch of billboards featuring 'Wal E, The Kajun Gator', and we fired up 'KAJUN 103.'

"Hi Paulsy!" was not on the billboards, just on this piece of art given to me by the designer.

Our debut rating book showed us with a six share. Six months later we had a ten share and six months after that, a thirteen share.

In our first full year WKJN became Baton Rouge's #1 Country station, with gross revenue of $1,859,089 ... an increase of 260% from where we started.

Note: After missing the chance to purchase KJUN for $1.7 million, we later bought it for $2.7 million. Some people thought we were nuts. Two years later we sold the station for $7 million in a 3-station deal.

WNNK – 'WINK 104'

Next up for us was a rare opportunity in Harrisburg, PA.

WTPA-FM was a full Class B FM (50 kw @ 500' HAAT) in a Rock format, rated #1 with Men 18 – 44. The station had annual revenue of $1.3 million and operating cash flow of $300,000. As I recall, the asking price for the station was $2.7 million.

The only other 'B' licensed to Harrisburg was WHP-FM. This station was owned by the *Harrisburg Patriot Newspaper,* virtually guaranteeing that it was being treated more as a 'bother' than an asset. At least, that's how it sounded.

The remaining competition was an assortment of small-footprint Class A FMs (3 kw @ 300' HAAT) and a handful of AM stations, plus another Class B, a really good sounding Country station licensed to Ephrata, PA, a town thirty-some miles south of Harrisburg.

Initially Kerby thought we should change WTPA's format to Country, believing that in a reasonably short period of time we could win in a head-to-head battle.

I, too, thought we would win such a battle, but given that we had several months before receiving our FCC grant I wanted to study the matter further, to see if there was a way we could change the format while retaining a decent portion of the station's sizable male audience. I was looking to stay in the ratings race and preserve much of the station's revenue, while avoiding the problems incurred in head-to-head battle.

Further analysis revealed the leading Top Forty station to be WKBO, a low-power AM station with very substantial ratings 'anchored' by their morning personality, Tim Burns, a major-market talent by any description.

This small footprint AM station was knocking the market dead at the same time that FM listenership was vaulting past AM.

Hmmm.

With that in mind I suggested we change the format to a rock-leaning Top Forty and add the imaging, promotions, and audience involvement that was by now our stock in trade. I believed that these changes would allow us to retain a lot of the station's revenue and half of the station's male audience, while adding a like number of female listeners. This balanced demographic of primarily 18 – 44 year-old adults would quickly get us in the ratings fight and keep the station in the position of being a viable 'buy' for regional and national ad agencies, even as the audience adjusted to the changes.

Kerby agreed. Then he added a huge kicker.

"I'm gonna get Tim Burns."

Apoplexy

Aboard on day one was an outstanding General Manager - the one and only Carol O'Leary (now Logan) – the first female GM to grace our company. Carol was a no-nonsense veteran broadcast executive with an extensive track record of success. 'Inheriting' Carol was 'Top Five' on the list of the best things that ever happened for us.

Note: She went on to become a station owner and CEO. She's still a good friend.

Shortly after the November closing, Kerby and I met with Carol to explain our plans to change the station format and imaging. At this Carol lit up another Salem cigarette and turned white as a ghost. She thought we were crazy to even *contemplate* changing anything.

Carol: "My God guys. We're on top of the world. We set new revenue records every month. Please...don't do this."

Us: "Mmm, Carol...you're on top of *your* world, but it's a world that's limited to males 18-44. We believe our changes will put you on top of *the* world."

A long conversation ensued, during which Carol lit additional Salems while expressing the fear that she'd lose her job.

"If this doesn't work I'll be the blame," she said.

"Not gonna happen," sez I. "If this *fails* it's on us. But when it <u>*succeeds*</u> - *that* will be on you. Ya gotta trust us."

As the color began to return to her face, Carol took a deep breath and crushed out her current cigarette.

"OK guys. What's next?"

(This lady is 'dead game'. I'm impressed!)

Every Sundae Needs A Cherry On Top

Kerby: "Oh yeah, I almost forgot. We're going to get Tim Burns."

Carol (incredulously): "You're gonna do *what*? Get Tim Burns? Mmm, I don't think so. He has a non-compete."

Kerb (smiling): "Step aside and let me work my magic.

To us, Tim Burns was 'The Franchise' for WKBO, with a huge following of listeners. We needed to get him outta there and onboard with us. His non-compete prevented him from working for an in-market competitor for a period of one year. On the 'QT' Kerby had been talking with Tim, even going so far as to suggest that, should WKBO try to enforce the non-compete, Tim could work at one of our other stations and return to Harrisburg a year later. (What a promotional opportunity *that* would be!)

As it turned out, Kerby negotiated a cash 'buy-out' of the non-compete and Tim was able to join us immediately. He was the on-air catalyst that made WINK 104 an instant success for decades, both in the ratings battle and the revenue wars.

Here's how Tim remembers it:

> *I anguished for weeks over moving to WNNK back in mid or late 1984. I remember most of it, Paul. The WKBO owner was happy with me. They were paying me a good salary with some nice perks. It's not easy to leave when you have a good relationship with your employer. Very easy to leave when you don't!*
>
> *Kerby contacted me and offered a higher salary. I reported back to the owner who said he'd match it. Then Kerby offered fifteen percent more, plus he also matched the four weeks of vacation time I'd earned, which I felt was very generous. The owner would not increase his offer.*
>
> *I mentioned to Kerby during a phone call that I had had numerous great offers in the past that never panned out. That was a turning point because he then promised to put it all in writing. Of course, that clinched it. I made the big decision. Never regretted it for one second.*
>
> *Kerby had asked me if I would consider going to work out of town for a year (to avoid a lawsuit over my non-compete) - I think it was somewhere down south. I wasn't keen on that. It didn't matter as it turned out. since Paul and Kerby negotiated a buy-out of the non-compete—somebody mentioned $1500, but I'm not certain. It was humbling since I never thought I was that good.*

I never had a clue that I would ever do as well in radio as I did at WINK 104. That's all thanks to you and Kerby.

That's how it all happened to the best of my memory.

The Roll-Out

To introduce 'The New WINK 104' we planned a giant party for 7 PM, Friday, January 18, 1985 in the ballroom of the Harrisburg Marriott—invitees to include as many clients and ad agency folks as we could muster. Call letters, format, Tim Burns...everything would be revealed at 9 PM that evening.

Sidebar: We didn't realize that January 18th was the date for the release of the ARBitron advances. Earlier that day we got our first look at the ratings from the Fall 1984 survey. WTPA had scored its highest ratings ever!

Carol lit another Salem!

"Damn the torpedoes. Full steam ahead."
—Rear Admiral David G. Farragut, U S Navy. Aug. 5, 1864

Hundreds of folks joined us for drinks, hors d'oeuvres and the big announcement, with a countdown to begin at 8:59:50 PM.

Radio people + ad agency people + clients = One Helluva Party!

Five...four...three...two...one ... BOOM!

At 9 PM WINK 104 was born.

Perspective: Getting Tim Burns was akin to the LA Lakers getting Shaquille O'Neal, the Houston Astros getting Justin Verlander, and Macy's signing an exclusive agreement with Oscar de la Renta. That big.

On any radio station, the morning show is the key building block for gathering audience share for the rest of the day. Tim was one of the best 'gatherers' in the business, on top of which he was a person of quality. He loved Harrisburg and he loved radio…and it showed.

Following Tim on the air was the mercurial (and, well…*very* controversial) Bruce Bond. Recalling his hijinks would require at least one stand-alone chapter in this book. If you are familiar with Harrisburg radio 1985-90 you know exactly what I mean.

When I was at WNNK I spent lots of time with Bruce. Let's just say he was a challenge. Talented, untamable, in a way unteachable…and very memorable. For a very long time he garnered huge ratings but eventually burned himself out.

Performance

It wasn't very long before 'Big Footprint WNNK' buried 'small-footprint WKBO' en route to becoming the #1 rated radio station in every important adult demographic, and the highest billing station in the market. This took just eighteen months.

Carol Logan was a great GM because she was a brilliant businessperson...and a wonderful colleague to boot. *(I'm thrilled to report that she quit smoking!)* The change of format worked quicker and better than we'd imagined.

Station revenue in 1984 was $1,450,000.00. Revenue after our first year (1985) was over $2,000,000.00, and in 1986, $2,700,000.00, and Carol looked great *sittin' on top o' the world.*

WIZD – 'WIZARD 104, The Wizard of the Gulf Coast'

The third of our three November '84 deals was an AM/FM combo licensed to Atmore, Alabama, population approximately 5,500.

With the exception of its really fun call letters - WSKR (WHISKER?), I don't remember much about the AM. Kerby reminded me that we sold it to a family of Mennonites. Legend has it that Manhattan was sold for trinkets and other swag valued at $24.00. That's probably more than we got for WSKR.

Note: Who better than a family of Mennonites to own a radio station called WHISKER? But I digress.

The FM is a different story.

WATM was a full Class C FM operating on a relatively short tower and covering a wide swath of that part of Alabama located between fifty and one-hundred miles north of the Gulf of Mexico, due north of Mobile, AL and Pensacola, FL and up where nobody lived. The stations were owned by Mr. Julius E. Talton of Selma, AL, a businessman of note and one of Alabama's most respected broadcasters.

With an FCC construction permit in hand, Mr. Talton had joined with two other FM broadcasters in a consortium to build 1,700 feet of steel in Locksley, AL, at the top of which would be affixed a triangular-shaped 'triplex'.

Each radio station would have a short antenna on one of the 'points' of the triangle @ 1600' HAAT, thus giving birth to three flame-throwing FM radio stations. One of the other broadcasters owned a station in Pensacola, the other a station in Mobile. Mr. Talton's station was a non-factor in either market.

Upon completion of the project, each of the FM stations would cover both Mobile and Pensacola like a blanket, effectively doubling the size of the potential audience and client base. (Going south over the Gulf of Mexico, the ultimate 'flat terrain', these three radio signals could be heard all the way to the curvature of the earth.)

Total cost of the project was $1,800,000.00.

Mr. Talton was asking $2.7-million for the radio stations. Firm.

Strip-Marketing Opportunity

We viewed this as the ideal strip-market opportunity. We'd be one of only three stations with 70dbu signal over both Mobile and Pensacola. All we needed to do was get the tower built and the antenna in place, choose a format, staff it up and watch it grow, right?

"Not so fast my friend."
—Lee Corso, College GameDay

Strip Marketing Reality

We learned the 'strip marketing' strategy early in our careers when we worked for Susquehanna Broadcasting, I at WSBA in York, PA and Kerby at WARM in Scranton, PA.

The idea was to acquire a large-footprint radio station that covered two or more otherwise separate markets, then use the strength of the station's signal to unite the markets under one name. *Example*: WSBA covered York, Lancaster and Harrisburg which WSBA named 'WSBA Land'. WARM covered Scranton, Wilkes-Barre and Hazleton. And Voila! 'WARMland'.

Given the popularity of the radio stations and the size of their audiences, it wasn't long before these names 'took root', making the stations an easy sell to those businesses seeking to become more regional in nature – and at top ad rates!

We used this strategy with WILQ, 'one-naming' the coverage area 'The Susquehanna Valley'. It was a smashing success. We viewed Mobile-Pensacola as a solid fit for this model.

Our research in Mobile-Pensacola revealed Hot AC to be 'the format hole' and our best choice for a format that would be competitive in both markets. For call letters we chose WIZD. *WIZARD 104 – The Wizard of the Gulf Coast*

We interviewed several people for the position of General Manager, eventually choosing Dennis Ryan, GM of an AM/FM in Atlantic City, NJ. This turned into an exceptional 'two-fer' when Dan Farr, Dennis' Sales Manager also joined us.

For our 'one-name' we co-opted 'The Gulf Coast'. Both Mobile and Pensacola were located there and besides…that's what everybody else was already calling it.

And awaay we went!

*Vivere Et Discere**

Short version: The first ratings showed us with really solid numbers in Pensacola whilst the Mobile numbers were lousy. Really lousy.

We were dumbfounded. This simply made no sense. The 'format hole' was the same in both markets. Why should it have worked in one place but not the other?

Acting out of disbelief (*denial?*) we 'doubled down' by aiming more on-air content at Mobile, but our early rating success in Pensacola mostly negated this effort because most of our advertisers were Pensacola businesses. To Mobileians, this only served to make us sound even more like a Pensacola station. The 'high in Pensacola, low in Mobile' ratings pattern continued.

Being a couple of hard-headed Pennsylvania German boys who were fully convinced that we were right, we continued in Winston Churchill mode: "We shall never, never, never give in"! Because our business model was built on making the station a strip market success we 'kept on keeping on'. We were absolutely stuck in that mode, failing to realize that we had a very successful Pensacola station and should have concentrated on Pensacola.

Drilling Deeper

What we failed to discover in our initial research is that, culturally speaking, the cities of Mobile, AL and Pensacola, FL could not have been further apart. See, the folks there didn't really like one another very much. We would too-late learn that Mobileians looked down their noses at Pensacola as 'that Navy town' while Pensacolans believed Mobileians to be a bunch of snobs.

Mobelians viewed their city as 'The Jewel of the South'.

Pensacolans knew they were having the most fun.

*Vivere et discere = Live and Learn

The cultural differences between these two markets made it impossible for the strip marketing strategy to work. Nevertheless, we were able to build the business to a respectable level.

Performance

Dan Farr put together and pre-sold an introductory package of advertising to begin when the WIZARD went on the air with the new antenna (May, 1985). April 1985 station revenue was $39,000.00. From May through December the average monthly revenue was $110,000.00.

Station revenue continued to grow but never reached the levels of our early forecast.

Strictly Business

As pointed out earlier, Mr. Julius Talton was a widely respected and very astute businessman. We were soon to learn why he richly deserved this reputation.

Consider: The morning of the closing at the station offices in Atmore, Mr. Talton was in attendance along with Kerby, me, and our lawyer, Bob Wright. The majority of the documents had been prepared in advance so the meeting was mostly about signing papers - lots and lots of papers.

The final detail was making sure that proper funds were transferred into Mr. Talton's bank account. A few minutes after the bank called with the assurance that $2.7 million dollars was in his account Mr. Talton stood and said, "Well gentlemen, I want to thank you for buying my radio stations. Now, my pretty wife and I are going to our place at Gulf Shores for the weekend. I wish y'all the very best of luck."

And with that, he and his 'pretty wife' rode his BMW into the sunset.

Getting' Outta Dodge

Around noon Kerby and I said our goodbyes to Dennis and headed for home. Around 2 PM the car phone rang. It was Dennis.

"So...you're not gonna believe this. Mr. Talton called about fifteen minutes ago. 'Dennis', he said, 'I need you to do me a favor. Please check the postage meter and let me know if there was anything left on it'.

"I checked and sure enough...the meter showed a balance of twenty-seven dollars and thirty five cents. I went back to the phone with that information, after which Mr. Talton said, 'I'd be appreciative if you could draw me a check for that amount and send it to me at my office. Thank you'.

"Credit Where It's Due

It's highly possible that if not for Dennis Ryan, this technical facility may never have been completed. Ok, Ok...I exaggerate. But it was Dennis' natural talent for organizing that finally got the job done, especially so where the building of the antenna was concerned.

It seemed like the other two owners felt no urgency regarding completion of the tower project. Dennis went after it like a cheetah in pursuit of a Thompson's gazelle. He made at least two trips to New England where the triplex was being assembled and spent hours on the phone with the tower and the antenna people, basically taking over administration and supervision of the project.

Hats off to Dennis. Dennis Martin Ryan passed away on May 21, 2012.

CHAPTER 17
MARCOM

Those of you who've played any sport are no doubt aware that in every contest you're not just playing against the other team (or person), you're also playing against the rules.

In football, for example, one of the most often called offensive penalties is that of 'holding'. The rules state that offensive players may not use their hands to grab and hold a defensive player. We also know the great offensive linemen have long-since developed 'skills' for committing undetected holds, thus 'successfully working the rules'.

In baseball, the great catchers know how to 'frame' pitches that are outside of the strike zone in such a way as to convince the umpire that the pitches were *inside* the strike zone, thus turning a pitch that would otherwise have been (properly) called 'ball two' into one that the umpire calls 'Stee-rike Three'.

So...what about businesses behaving in ways that are unquestionably *within the rules* (regulations? laws?) as written (words have meanings) - but that regulators would most probably go out of their way to interpret as being outside the *intent* of the rules.

'Working the rules' if you will, or more properly the *lawyers' domain.*

Welcome To 1985

The Federal Communications Commission (FCC) has an encyclopedia of rules and regulations governing broadcast ownership. Broadcasters caught acting outside the rules subject themselves to severe penalties, everything from large cash fines to loss of licenses. Broadcast owners know: 'Violate the rules at your own peril'.

FCC rules circa 1985 stated that no broadcast owner, whether an individual or a corporation, could *control* the licenses of more than fourteen radio stations – seven AM and seven FM – with the operative word being 'control'. So the question becomes, "What are the conditions precedent that constitute control"? Broadly speaking, any person or entity owning 50.01% (or more) of any radio station would be deemed by the FCC to be 'in control' of that license.

Note: broadcasters do not own the licenses – they are owned by the 'public'.

One section of every license application is a series of pages that detail for the FCC exactly who will own controlling interest in the company holding the license - names, addresses, percentage of voting stock, etc., as well as a list of other licenses that are controlled by the applicant.

We found ourselves in the position of being 'maxed-out' at seven FM licenses...sad, because the brokers kept calling us with really good opportunities, some of which were in small or medium markets.

What to do, what to do?

Who Do You Trust?

Short version: We decided to create a new company, Marcom, Inc., to be in control of the licenses of these smaller-market stations.

We set up in a location separate from Keymarket, and brought Marshall Magee to Augusta from Jackson, MS to be Marcom's President. Marshall would own 100% of the voting stock of Marcom, which was ten percent of *all* company stock.

Ninety percent of the company stock was non-voting, so by definition the owners of that stock were deemed to be not in control. Kerby and I owned the non-voting stock. We lined up the financing to purchase these stations, but Marshall had absolute control of the licenses.

Note: We trusted Marshall 100%. He never gave us any reason whatsoever to doubt the wisdom of that decision. When we ran this by Shrinsky he said, "I get what you're saying but I strongly recommend against. Don't do this." (Actually Jason was apoplectic. We moved forward.)

In the category of 'how times change', The Communications Act of 1996 made what we did in 1986 look like child's play. By 2005 Clear Channel owned over 1,200 radio stations in America.

Next Up

Marcom purchased KZBB, Curt Van Loon's Class C FM licensed to Poteau, OK but doing business in Ft. Smith, AR – in an Adult Contemporary format. The station was alone in its format and had decent ratings. It was doing pretty OK – a nice acquisition for us.

Curt called one day with the following story: It seems there was a former owner of the station who was owed some money from an installment sale he'd made to the owner-operator from whom Curt had purchased the station – that's two sales before we got involved.

The guy had been working Curt over for the money, claiming that Curt had assumed this obligation when he purchased the station...which would have been true if Curt had purchased the *stock* of that company, but Curt had purchased the assets.

The guy had been threatening Curt who, despite best efforts, had been unable to change this fella's mind. The guy was dead set on getting his money. So Curt's in his office in Ft. Smith when he gets a call from someone living near the transmitter site over in Poteau, OK.

"You need to get over here quick. Some idiot is out by one of your guy anchors. He's got a hack saw and he's sawing away at the guy wires. Ya better do something soon or your tower's gonna fall."

Curt called the Sheriff and headed to Poteau. By the time he arrived the Sheriff had the situation under control with minimal damage.

The guy was livid but there was nothing he could do.

Just another day in the radio biz.

Note: Radio stations are federally licensed. As such, anyone charged and convicted of tampering with a radio station is guilty of a Federal Crime.

Rounded On Both Ends And 'Hi' In The Middle

Then there was WZOQ-FM, '92 ZOO' licensed to Wapakoneta, OH, home of Astronaut and U S Senator John Glenn, the first American to orbit the earth.

This Hot Top Forty station was a Class A FM (3-kw @ 300' HAAT) that covered Lima, a tidy and prosperous little market in western Ohio...all in all a very nice opportunity.

The seller was John Bulmer, one of the smartest cleverest, most interesting young broadcasters I ever met. He reminded me of Kerby and me 'from earlier years'. John's '92 ZOO' had stared down two cannons – a powerful heritage AM station and its 50-kw FM companion – and took his 3-kw 'pea shooter' FM to the top of the ratings.

Impressive. Marcom bought the station.

Leap Froggin'

Next was an opportunity on a full Class B FM (50-kw @ 500' HAAT) licensed to Utica, NY.

Utica/Rome, NY was not among the more prosperous markets in the northeast, but the price was right, the footprint was huge...and no station was playing Country music, by that time America's fastest-growing format.

Oh...and Dan Farr (WIZD Sales Manager) was born and raised in Utica. This one was a 'natural' for Marcom.

Dan was elevated to the position of GM, the call letters were changed to WFRG and Presto! The FROGGY imaging campaign was born.

The Froggy face! Created by Dan Farr

Note: WFRG would become the most successful of the Marcom stations.

...And More

The brokers kept feeding us opportunities. Davenport, IA and Bangor, ME come to mind.

But the strangest and craziest deal we ever did – Marcom, Keymarket, whatever – came when we agreed to purchase a station that was licensed to Ottawa, KS, but was holding a construction permit to build a tower and relocate their antenna to serve all of Topeka and Lawrence, KS.

Background: When a broadcaster makes an application to change antenna locations that includes the construction of a new tower, permission to build that tower must be gained by applying to the Federal Aviation Agency ("FAA") as well as applicable local government agencies. In many cases, finding a site that gives the broadcaster the precise added territory he wishes to cover, and at the same time complies with FCC requirements re station-to-station spacing, can be very difficult.

In other words, 'ya can't just put it any old place'.

In this case there was but one spot for us to build the tower and hang the antenna...and gain the coverage of Topeka and Lawrence we were seeking. That spot was some nine miles from the Topeka airport, more or less in direct alignment with one of their runways.

It was 'build it there or don't build it at all'.

All required local approvals and permits had been granted and FAA approval received. We were awaiting our FCC grant before beginning construction... ...when all hell broke loose.

The sudden 'last minute' firestorm was furious, eventually including Senator Robert Dole who (we heard) had contacted the FAA to officially protest their decision to approve the application.

Enjoy the newspaper articles as well as a massively circulated 'hand out', plus some comedy from Scott Davis, the station's General Manager.

Radio tower site causes stir

By PAM MILLER
Staff writer

A couple of clowns were walking around Lawrence and the KU campus yesterday.

But they weren't clowning around. They were serious.

In another part of town, a radio station vice president sat in his office, and he, too, was serious.

The clowns and the vice president represent opposite sides of a controversy.

The clowns were Topeka residents, Jim Woods and Pauline Beatty, who protested the future installment of a

Highly Recommended: For news clippings and other fun stuff from the fire storm of controversy, download our companion PDF.

http://www.rlpublishers.com/WWW_companion.pdf

We weathered the storm and the tower was built.

As 1985 was coming to an end, Keymarket owned seven FM and four AM stations.

Marcom was in control of seven FM's and five AM's.

And two gigantic deals were on the horizon.

CHAPTER 18
THE BIG LEAGUES

November of 1985 saw us take a giant step forward.

CHAPMAN ASSOCIATES
MAJOR MARKET DIVISION

N E W S L E T T E R

Edited and Published by Charles Giddens, Chapman Associates Major Market Division 1255 23rd Street, NW, Suite 890, Washington, DC 20037 (202) 822-8913

November, 1985

The Big Deals Get Bigger

Kerby Confer and Paul Rothfuss' Keymarket Group buys Joe Amaturo's KMJQ, Houston, KMJM, St. Louis and WLTI, Detroit for $65 million.

Keymarket sells WKJN, Hammond (Baton Rouge) LA, WMSI Jackson, MS and WSSL Grey Court (Greenville) SC and two AM's to Larry Patrick's new Sterling Communications for $24 million.

I think it was the June 1985 AIMS meeting when famed broadcast entrepreneur and philanthropist, Joe Amaturo, told us he'd made a deal to sell his stations in Houston, St. Louis and Detroit for a very large sum. There were congratulations all around, after which we went back to the business of the meeting.

Case closed, right?

Nope.

By summer's end Joe's deal had cratered and he was looking for a buyer.

The Amaturo Deal

At Rosemary Hall our desks faced one another, some forty feet apart across a wide and spacious first-floor hallway, all part of a large and totally open office space — a huge departure from our first office together some ten years earlier in Williamsport, where shared a 12' x 12' room with our desks pushed together, back-to-back.

In either case it was almost impossible not to hear parts of each others phone conversations, and we'd use hand signals if one needed the other's attention.

(How's that for sophisticated inter-office communication!)

One August afternoon Kerby was on the phone with Joe Amaturo, who was lamenting the loss of his deal and asking if Kerb had any ideas about companies that might be interested buyers. At some point in the conversation I overheard Kerby tell Joe that he couldn't think of anyone who might be a buyer.

I hand-signaled Kerby and mouthed, *"How about us"?*

Kerby asked Joe the question and the hunt was on.

Short version: We employed the services of the Connecticut investment banking firm of Joel Hartstone and Barry Dickstein (H & D) to pull together the financing for us. H & D was a very successful investment banking company. A trip or two to CT had us laying out a strategy for raising the financing, and joining Joel and Barry in meetings with potential bankers and investors.

Thanks to Joel and Barry the financing was pulled together very quickly.

In November we signed the purchase agreement and filed the FCC application; the former buyer sued Amaturo for Specific Performance based on a Letter of Intent the parties had previously signed; this led Amaturo to negotiate with the 'jilted suitor'; which led to a settlement whereby Amaturo paid several million dollars to drop the suit, and that same amount was added to our purchase price.

Just another day at the office. Here are the complete details of the deal, as meticulously described in Paul Kagan's Newsletter dated July 11, 1986.

BROADCAST
BANKER/BROKER

No. 27

July 11, 1986

Paul Kagan Associates, Inc.
126 Clock Tower Place
Carmel, California 93923-8734
(408) 624-1536

KEYMARKET CLOSES KEY DEAL

Temporarily derailed by a lawsuit against the seller, Keymarket Communications' purchase of FMs in Houston, Detroit and St. Louis from the Amaturo Group took seven months to close and ended up costing $1.35 mil. more than was originally planned.

Not to worry however, as principals Kerby Confer and Paul Rothfuss are picking up the three major-market positions for $61.45 mil. At 7.2x first-year cash flow, in a fully bootstrapped deal investment-banked by another inimitable pair – Hartstone and Dickstein.

The deal was inked with Amaturo last December for the #1 FM in Houston, a money bleeder with a 50% margin; a steady #4 in St. Louis; and a non-performing #18 in Detroit. Since then, WLTI (Detroit) has switched (formats) to Transtar 41 from EZ-vocal and rocketed from a 1.8% audience (share) to a 3.4 in the recent ratings. KMJQ Houston, despite the stagnating economy there, is holding position and billing slightly better than last year.

Keymarket is looking for $12 million in revenue and $6 million in cash flow from Houston through 6/87; $4 mil. and $1.5 mil from KMJM St. Louis; and $3.25 mil. and $1 mil. from Detroit.

Detroit's quick turnaround and Houston's endurance have really helped to highlight Keymarket's bargain in an era of 10x-cash-flow radio station sales. What really makes the deal shine, however, is that it was done with no cash.

Keymarket raised $66.35 mil. for purchase and working capital - $46.25 mil. of sr. secured funds, $10 mil. of jr. notes, and the balance of $10 mil. in subordinated seller paper divided into a $4 mil. seller note at 11% (half ballooned), a $3.1 mil. consultancy, and a $3 mil. non-compete agreement, each payable over five years.

The senior lenders are John Hancock, Equitable and Massachusetts Mutual, which took $23 mil. at 11 1/8% over ten years; and BayBank Boston, Bank of New York, and Fleet, which took $23 mil. at prime + 1 ¾%, decreasing to prime + 1 ¼% once the debt-to-cash flow ratio drops to 5.25x.

Bridge Capital and Equitable Capital split the jr. funding, which carries a 10% current coupon and kicker warrants intended to provide those investors with a 30% compounded return over five years.

Assuming Keymarket could turn around and sell its new trio for 9x 1987 cash flow - a not unreasonable expectation - there's a quick $15 mil. profit to be made, and an infinite return on investment for the sweat equity holders.

Such an immediate step-up in value obviously bodes well for the five-year ROI results the venturers can anticipate.

—

Unintended Consequences Can Be Wonderful

This stellar deal, as praised by Kagan, comes straight from our 'Timing Is Everything' department.

Without the aforementioned lawsuit bugaboo, the deal that was signed in November 1985 would have closed in April of 1986. The unexpected delay led to a huge 'up' for us.

Consider: In 1985 radio stations were trading in multiples of seven-to-ten times operating cash flow, but cash flow was not always the only factor to affect a sale price. Ofttimes the format of the station was also a serious consideration.

Example: Selling a Country station with a large audience in the 25-54 age demographic will cause the sale multiple to be on the high side, while a smaller audience, higher age demographic, beautiful music station would most probably make the sale multiple much lower.

Our asset purchase agreement was signed in late 1985, a time when radio stations in Urban formats traded at the lower end of the multiple scale.

Why?

Conventional Wisdom (CW) presumed the audience of an Urban station to be primarily African-American. This audience was also presumed to be comparatively economically deprived. As such, the station's revenue-growth potential was viewed as 'compromised' because the poorer audience would have less money to spend on the products being advertised, making it more difficult for many businesses to justify running their ads on Urban stations.

(Hey! Don't blame me. I'm just the messenger.)

By mid-1986, however, the CW had flipped and Urban stations were now trading in higher multiples. Broadcasters now reasoned that no one would choose an Urban format if other formats were available, meaning if you owned a successful Urban station you would be alone in the format and without competition!

The result?

In the time between our signing [Nov. 1985] and the closing {July 1, 1986}, the estimated value of the two Urban stations – KMJQ (Houston) and KMJM (St. Louis) – had increased from seven times cash flow to nine times cash flow, an on-paper increase in value of some $14 million dollars.

Clearly a case of 'right place, right time'.

Detroit

In August, I made a trip to Detroit to get acquainted with the management and staff of WLTI.

WLTI in Detroit was in an EZ Vocal format: Steve Lawrence, Frank Sinatra, Eydie Gorme', Nat 'King' Cole, Patti Page, Steve Lawrence and Eydie Gorme'...you get the idea. We had no plans whatsoever to exchange this for an expensive format battle with a market-leading Country station or AC station or Rock station. WLTI was Lite 99 and LITE 99 it was going to stay.

I was met at the airport by Jeff Sleete, WLTI's General Manager and a very impressive young man. His excitement was evident as he told me about the latest ARBitron ratings, showing WLTI with an increase from a 1.8 to a 3.2.

"That's good," I said. "Congratulations. But please Jeff, don't get yourself worked up about the ratings. I can assure you I won't be. They're too low to be noticed by the ad agencies anyway, so in reality, they don't matter.

"To me here's what matters. You have a good-sized audience of mostly upper-income adults. What you have to do is identify those local businesses that want to reach that audience and present the station to them directly. Along the way you'll get some agency business but that will be gravy. Local-direct business is the key.

Please...concentrate on local-direct business. You'll do great and we'll both be very happy. I don't think it's worth worrying about ratings. You shouldn't either."

Note: The last I heard, Jeff Sleete was the VP of Sales Research for Sinclair TV.

The 'Formula'

The Amaturo deal was a really BIG deal for us. In its size and strength and its power backing it was also a benchmark of sorts – one that certified the innate wisdom and blind luck of our unwritten plan and our 'fire-ready-aim' approach to radio.

When you think 'plan' you tend to think of a thoroughly researched and meticulously documented road map.

Not!

Our Plan? Prior to purchasing our first stations (1975) Kerby and I made a mental list of conditions we needed to have in place before considering an acquisition.

Condition #1

The station's broadcast signal (its 'footprint') must be equal to or better than the best signal in the market or we're not interested. Here's how we came to understand the importance of Rule #1.

The 'Top Forty' format developed in the early 1950s after TV took radio's programming. In many markets this 'new format' was first tried by lower powered (small-footprint) radio stations, but when these stations started showing ratings success the format was often co-opted by large footprint stations, cinching the demise of the small stations.

This strategy has been credited to legendary broadcaster Todd Storz who said, "Give me inferior programming and a superior signal and I'll whip your a$$."

What if you provided superior programming?

'Superior signal, superior programming' was our Key Rule.

The Rest of our 'Rules'

#2. There must be a 'format hole' in the market, or at least a 'weak-sounding' station in a primary format.

#3. If current station management is inadequate we must have 'our team' in mind before moving forward.

#4. Stations located in state capitals or in towns with large universities are 'bonus markets' and prime targets. These 'rules' were the keys we used to decide whether a market was right for us. Ergo "Keymarket," the name of our company.

The Method to the Madness

On August 1, 1975 (Day One) we believed we knew how to do this and with each new acquisition we'd backed our belief by putting everything we had on the table. But on that day did we absolutely positively know how to do this?

No.

From 1976 through 1981 we put our knowledge and everything we had on the line in the belief that it would work - an 'experiment in action' if you will.

With each successful re-imaging we gained confidence. We came to 'know what we knew' and how to implement same. Our actions bore this out. We'd developed a method or 'formula' without realizing that this was happening.

Our proven early successes - WILQ (1976), KSSN (1979) and WSSL (1981) led to our financing agreement with TA Associates, which enabled the rapid growth of Keymarket Communications.

None of this was in writing. We just bought 'em and got busy.

The "Formula" In Action

"Ya gotta get noticed."

To successfully re-image a radio station we concluded that we needed a 'hook' to make it easy for people to notice. Often this started with call letters.

We inherited WILQ but called it 'Q – 105' or simply 'The Q' - sorta cool and easy to remember.

Then there was WHUM – "I HUM IN MY CAR" (a great bumper sticker). KSSN - "96 KISSIN". WSSL - 'Whistle 100 – "I WSSL IN MY TRUCK". WIGL- 'I WIGL IN MY CAR'. WNNK - 'WINK 104'. And more.

Promotions were easily tied to these memorable 'names'.

We inherited and trained and/or hired great people. We shared the grand plan and when we were sure that they 'got it' - we got out of their way.

In every way and at every opportunity we got our stations out of the studio and into the community. Literally.

Using our on-air personalities, our station characters (The WILQ Rooster for example) and our management staff and team we tried to emulate the breadth of our on-air signal (which was everywhere) by physically being…everywhere.

While our competitors were 'busy with busy work' we were capturing franchises by becoming 'The Sponsoring Stations' for public and private events. Sports and art expos, theatre shows, charity events, county and township carnivals and fairs, community fireworks displays, etc. Occasionally our 'character' would stand on a street corner to just wave and greet folks passing by.

Whether paid for or done for free, wherever there were people either having fun or in need – there we were.

And we worked side-by-side with our clients producing events they created or that we conjured up for them.

The Thumbnail

All radio stations are not created equal. Buy only those with large footprints.

Do everything legally possible to get your stations noticed.

Develop great colleagues. Clue 'em in to 'the plan'. Train 'em. Step back and watch 'em flourish.

Your signal covers big geography. Get your station and staff out in it. Your on-air sound gets you one of the five senses – hearing. When you get out of the stations you get at least two more: sight, and touch. (If at a fair or expo you could get credit for taste and smell.) Three is always more than one.

There are more details. Most are minute in comparison.

If indeed this was the 'formula' for our success it sure worked great for Kerby and me.

It's still working today.

CHAPTER 19
SAYING GOODBYE

In the almost thirty years we worked together Kerby and I never had what you could call 'an argument'. I believe this is because we respected each-others' intelligence and experience and we never for a minute doubted the motive behind an opinion, even if we disagreed with that opinion.

Just prior to the purchase of our first radio stations we made the following pact: When it comes to very important decisions, if both votes are not 'yes' – it's a 'no'.

Oh…and the only 'working contract' we ever had was a handshake.

To say this was a highly unusual partnership would be a gross understatement.

Our partnership was a blessing...but we were not 'the same person.'

Right or wrong, my view was that we were handling our corporate responsibilities perfectly well, but in two different ways. For Kerby, Priority #1 was the business. For me, not so much. And for whatever reason, I became more and more concerned about this.

I-20 To Augusta

A nice April afternoon in 1986 found the two of us enjoying conversation while driving back to our office following a day at B-106 in Columbia, SC.

Why I chose this moment to 'speak up' I'll never know.

Out of the blue I said, “So I gotta ask you something. Are we doing OK”?

"What do you mean”? (Kerby seemed surprised by the question.)

“Are you and I OK...with each other”?

“I have no idea what you’re talking about.”

“I think you’re working harder than me,” I said. “Which, if that is the case, is unfair to you.”

Kerby said, “Relax. We’re doing fine.”

Loo’-Ah-Vuhl

A week or so later Barbie, and I were invited to join some friends in Louisville, KY in a finish-line box at Churchill Downs...for the Kentucky Derby. That visit would stir up dreams in me, dreams that had long lay dormant.

Note: The Derby completed the ‘Old Guy Trifecta’ for me. I met President Reagan in March (age 75), saw Jack Nicklaus win the Masters in April (age 46) and watched ‘Ferdinand’ (age 3) win the Derby with Bill Shoemaker in the irons (age 54).

Loving Horses

My father, Dr. Paul Arndt Rothfuss, *(‘P.A.’ to his friends)* was born in 1893 and raised on a large family farm in North-Central Pennsylvania. The fourth-born of nine children, by age seven he was the ‘horse boy’, responsible for the care and feeding of the working horses that pulled the family’s buggies, wagons and plows.

He fell in love with horses.

As a student at the University Of Maryland Medical School in Baltimore, *P.A.* discovered Pimlico Race Course, where he saw Man 'O War win the Preakness in 1921.

He fell in love with *Thoroughbred* horses.

By the time I came along in 1940 my Dad had his mind made up to have a farm and Thoroughbreds.

Starting when I was not yet three, Dad would sit me on the left arm of his easy chair and we'd go through the Stallion Register.

Each page featured pictures of the great racehorses that were at stud, mostly in Kentucky. Dad had a story about almost all of them.

I fell in love with Thoroughbred horses.

The Seed

In April of 1948 Dad took me with him to Maryland and the Janon Fisher Farm where (if memory serves) the Maryland stallion 'Swashbuckler' was at stud, a horse that Dad wanted to see.

First off, spring starts to arrive in Maryland in March, and by April it's in full bloom. That was the case at the Fisher farm, which to my young eyes was something that appeared to have stepped out of a magazine. That vision was still with me when, as adults in 1963, Barbie and I moved to Maryland.

We often took our children on rides around Baltimore County where it seemed as though a beautiful horse farm was always just around the next turn. A thought began to form: "I'd really like to have something like this someday."

'Annd...They're Off'

Aiken, SC was/is the site of many Thoroughbred training centers, primarily specializing in preparing young race horses for their debuts at major race tracks all over America.

We lived in Aiken. Why not us? Some time in June I convinced Barbie that we should get a couple of yearlings and try our luck. We had the money so why not.

A friend introduced me to Dr. Glenna Salyer, a mostly non-practicing veterinarian who owned a company that served as an agent for people buying or selling horses, and as a marketing firm for the sale of stallion shares.

I called Dr. Salyer and explained what Barbie and I wanted to do. In September of 1986 we met in Lexington where we went over the sale catalogs together and selected some yearlings to look at, and perhaps to buy.

With Glenna's help we bought three colts and a filly, which I had shipped to a farm in Aiken to be broken and started on their way to the races.

Now each day began around 8:00 AM with a trip to the farm to spend an hour or so observing the proceedings, after which I went to our office at Rosemary Hall.

And the love affair intensified.

Note: Glenna knew the horse business very well. I knew a lot about horses but the horse business? I was a novice and 'ripe for the plucking'. Glenna not only kept me out of trouble, she became a dear friend.

A Bolt Of Lightning

Each year we had a meeting with our lenders and venture capital partners, always in an impressively decorated and beautifully paneled conference room at the offices of a Boston law firm – a firm with more than fifty names on the letterhead.

A really big firm.

We were always required to present our personal financial statements to the lawyers as part of the information that documented the fact that we were behaving ourselves – 'due diligence' if you will.

At some point one of the lawyers was looking over my financial statement, which showed me with a net worth in the low eight figures.

"Wow," he said. "You're worth a lot of money."

Without emotion I replied, "Yeah...I guess so."

The lawyer sat upright, as if he'd been buzzed by lightning. "Yuh...ya...you don't seem impressed. This is *really good.*"

I said, "Well...of course I'm *happy* about it. But to me it's just a number on a piece of paper."

He seemed about to protest as I continued.

"There's never a day that I wake up thinking about my net worth. I'm *conscious* of it, but it's not my motivation.

"I'm motivated by the opportunity to work with a great partner in planning ways to turn around another 'dog' radio station and bring career opportunities to the young colleagues we always find there. The money that results is a byproduct of this effort. So yeah, to me it's just a number on a piece of paper."

By now my lawyer friend was shaking his head in disbelief. No doubt he was thinking, *"Who IS this guy? Is he off his rocker"?*

This moment with the lawyer served to direct my thinking down an errant path. Previous to that meeting I'd given little thought to my Net Worth...but when I measured it against my salary (with which I had no complaints) I realized that if I had that Net Worth in cash in a bank earning just five percent, I'd be taking home over three times as much money as my salary was producing.

Correct mathematics is emotionless and it never lies. But taking it by itself with no consideration of other factors is a gross over-simplification that can lead to bad decisions.

I came to learn that "just a number on a piece of paper" was one of those gross over-simplifications.

Into The Sunset

The more time I spent with my yearlings the more I yearned to spend more time with them. Within a month that yearning had reached a fever pitch.

I began to realize that the horses were distracting me from giving full attention to my responsibilities with Keymarket. This added to my established angst re 'Kerby working harder than I'.

Many factors were whirling about in my mind, one of which was fairness. For me to be occupied with anything not called Keymarket Communications would be a serious injustice to Kerby, to say nothing of our colleagues and investors.

I also came to believe, though we never discussed it, that Kerby would prefer to focus on larger markets when pursuing future acquisitions.

And those long-dormant visions of the Janon Fisher Farm had been reawakened.

After much personal agonizing and many long conversations with Barbie, I decided to ask Kerby to buy me out. We concluded that process, professionally and peacefully, in early January of 1987. I bought two-hundred acres of land just south of Aiken, SC, and began making plans to build a horse farm, the picture of which I'd been carrying around in my mind for almost forty years.

Beginning with my first day in radio (1958) I never viewed my career as 'work'. For seventeen years on the air I was paid good money to play records and say funny stuff – a miracle. Then Kerby and I acted on our boyhood pledge, took what we'd learned together, on-air and hands-on in radio broadcasting, and shared it with folks at poorly operated radio stations by introducing them to "Show Business." It truly was *Paul & Kerby's Great Adventure*.

# #

EPILOGUE

It was 1960...March I believe.

Kerby and I were working at WHGB in Harrisburg, PA. I worked nights - 7 PM to 1 AM. Kerby was doing afternoons. There was a problem.

Kerby's wife was expecting. The anticipated delivery date was 'yesterday'. Kerby's car was sitting on the 'island' parking lot located in the middle of the Susquehanna River. The car was out of gas and Kerb was out of money, living in fear that the baby would be coming but he'd have no way to get his wife to the hospital for the delivery.

My car had gas but I couldn't give it to Kerby. I needed it to get to work and back.

We implemented the following plan: Kerby would work his afternoon hours at the station and hang around while I did the same. If the baby started to come he'd take the car and get his wife to the hospital, come back and take me home and return to the hospital. If not, he'd drive me home when my show was over and take my car.

If the baby came he'd have transportation. If not he'd pick me up the next afternoon, we'd put gas in his car and he'd be in business.

I'll never forget that evening seeing Kerby around midnight, asleep on one of the office desks, waiting for me to wrap it up so he/we could go home.

No baby was coming when I signed the station off the air. Kerby dropped me off and went home. I went to bed.

Later that morning I got the news. "It's a boy"!

Sometime around noon we took a one gallon can, filled it with gasoline, put the gasoline in Kerby's car, and 'Vrooom'!

He had a son. We had our cars. All was right with the world.

During the nearly three decades we worked together there was a hiccup or two, but basically this is how it was.

From making a vow to someday co-own a radio station, to the years we ran 'record hops' together, to the years we learned sales and management together, to the years we actually co-owned radio stations together; Kerby Confer and I were business partners for thirty years. We've been friends for sixty-five.

Our partnership was built on respect for, and faith in, one another's motives and judgment...and a handshake.

We built a company on these pillars, to which I'd also add a deep love for the radio industry, dedication to our goal, and belief in our assemblage of fine colleagues.

Along the way I remember three stand-out 'Moments of Significance'.

The first was in the fall of 1958 when at age eighteen we made 'The Vow'. We never let it out of our sight.

The second Moment of Significance was August of 1972 when Kerby called me with a challenge. "So...where's the guy who wanted to own a radio station"?

A few days later (Labor Day weekend, 1972) Kerby offered me the 'opportunity' to take a 50% pay cut, come to WYRE in Annapolis, do the morning show and sell the rest of the day. "Ya gotta know the business end of a business if ya wanna run the business," he said.

I accepted the offer.

The third Moment of Significance was Fall, 1984.

No tables were available when around 7 PM, en route home from a business trip and w/o reservations, we showed up at the fancy Green Jacket Restaurant in Augusta, GA. We were invited to grab a seat in the lobby (we were not alone).

"The wait will be at least thirty minutes."

Somehow our conversation turned to radio station call letters. *(Imagine that!)*

East of the Mississippi most all radio station call signs begin with a 'W'. West of the river it's a 'K'. Work with me here: Go ahead and think of several sets of call letters that you absolutely know will never be used on any radio station.

ANYWAY, we each grabbed a pen and some paper napkins and began writing down would-be call letters, while also whispering the slogans and 'liners' we'd use as accompaniment, most of which I would never mention in polite company. Here's a mild one to get you started. WIPE.

See? You can just imagine what came into our minds.

In no time the two of us – two neatly-dressed forty-something 'businessmen' sitting in the lobby of a fancy restaurant – were bent over in our chairs, laughing hysterically.

After five or six minutes we started to settle down, at which point, through a stifled laugh, I said to Kerby, “By the way, *this* is how we earn our living.”

We made eye contact and were off again.

At its roots radio is ‘show business’, so in retrospect I think I was right. Remember ‘getting noticed’? Great call letters and great graphics made all of how we earned our keep so much easier.

I’m indebted to radio. It gave me all of its secrets and it also gave me colleagues and associates galore; relationships that I treasure, many of which cover parts of seven decades.

(Seven decades? How is that possible? I’m only thirty three!)

During my fifty-plus years in radio I ‘worked’ perhaps a total of fifteen days. The rest of it was pure joy – and a wonderful blessing.

Every day I found myself surrounded by proud, creative, and yes… kinda zany folks. Professionally speaking, radio was my heaven.

To paraphrase the Beach Boys: “I had Fun, Fun, Fun, ‘til someone took the stations away.”

I miss it every day.

THANK YOU

Many thanks for reading a story that, to me, is living evidence of the existence of 'The American Dream'. If I could achieve these heights in a field that I loved, and do so simply because I loved it, anyone can do likewise.

I've been blessed with the presence of many fine mentors: My parents, Dr. Paul A. Rothfuss and Maria Duncombe Rothfuss; my high school English teacher Mrs. Rose Harer; Mr. Paul Warnick, Dean of Boys at Williamsport High School; AI Saunders, Robert C. Hazard, Flo Ayres, Marvin Schein, Marvin Mirvis, Dick Chapin, Mel Blanc, and Earl Nightingale. And James and Dorothy Love.

And one brilliant business partner – Kerby E. Confer.

'Thank you' to businesses that provide entry level jobs to young people, especially to Dave Castlebury. In hiring me he must have figured that at $0.8S/hour I couldn't do much damage.

I knew nothing. Dave gave me a shot.

I found a career.

If you're a young person, or if you know one, tell them to treat their minimum wage job with respect. It's an opportunity to get a toe-hold...to learn the value of excellent performance and how to work with others. Love it. Work hard. Excel. Move up.

Special thanks to Barbara Allen Love, my bride of sixty years - plus three years of 'going steady'. She was Barbie before there was 'Barbie'.

To our marriage, Barbie brought a constitution of stainless steel and an unbending devotion to me, the likes of which I suspect few men ever get to experience.

Barbie loves opera, great books, football (Yaaay!), and especially our family. And... ulp!...time spent with me.

Plus she can cook!

Bless you, my Sweet Darling. You make life worth living.

APPENDIX

Radio Stations Purchased/Operated/Re-imaged

WILQ, Williamsport, PA (Q 105) — Country

WLYC, Williamsport, PA – 'The Music of Your Life'

WHUM, Reading, PA — Country

WNOZ, Cortland, Ithaca, NY (The Nose) — Rock *

KSSN, Little Rock, AR (96 Kissin') — Country *

WSSL, Greenville, SC (Whistle 100) — Country *

WMSI, Jackson, MS (MISS 103) — Country

WJDX, Jackson, MS (62JDX) — News/Talk

WIGL, Orangeburg/Columbia, SC (Wiggle 106) — Country *

WTCB, Columbia, SC (B-106) — Adult Contemporary

WNNK, Harrisburg, PA (WINK 104) — Rock-leaning Top 40 *

WKJN, Baton Rouge, LA (Kajun 104) — Country *

WIZD, Mobile, AL/Pensacola, FL (Wizard 104) — Hot AC *

WBVR, Russellville, KY (The Beaver) — Country *

WFFX, Tuscaloosa, AL (The Fox) — Hot AC

WZNY, Augusta, GA (Sunny 105) — AC ^

KHUM, Ottawa, KS (Lawrence/Topeka) – Country*

WFRG, Utica, NY (Froggy) — Country

WPIG, Olean, NY (The Big Pig) — Country

WNKI, Elmira/Corning, NY (WINK) — Hot AC

WPGI, Elmira, NY (Piggie) — Country

WBZD, Williamsport, PA (OldieZ 93) — Oldies

Radio stations that Kerby Confer and I (or me alone) bought, re-imaged and turned into top rated stations. Many are still #1 in their formats.

*= built tall tower

^= relocated antenna

#

Contact The Author:
mailto: Paul@RLPublishers.com

Follow Paul "Emperor" Rodgers on Facebook:
https://www.facebook.com/phdwriter/

See more from Paul "Rodgers" Rothfuss at:
http://emperorrodgers.com/

Enlist in Rodger's Royal Commandos:
http://emperorrodgers.com/Commandos.html

Download a separate PDF file of the images and links contained in this book:
http://www.rlpublishers.com/WWW_companion.pdf

#

Made in the USA
Middletown, DE
03 July 2020